CONTEMPORARY
BIBLICAL
INTERPRETATION
FOR
PREACHING

CONTEMPORARY BIBLICAL INTERPRETATION FOR PREACHING

RONALD J. ALLEN

Judson Press® Valley Forge

CONTEMPORARY BIBLICAL INTERPRETATION FOR PREACHING
Copyright © 1984
Judson Press, Valley Forge, PA 19482-0851

The Bible quotations in this publication are from the Revised Standard Version of the Bible copyrighted 1946, 1952 © 1971, 1973 by the Division of Christian Education of the National Council of the Churches of Christ in the U.S.A., and used by permission.

Library of Congress Cataloging in Publication Data
Allen, Ronald J.
  Contemporary biblical interpretation for preaching.

  Includes bibliographical references and index.
  1. Bible—Homiletical use—Addresses, essays, lectures.   2. Preaching—Addresses, essays, lectures.   3. Bible—Criticism, interpretation, etc.—History—20th century—Addresses, essays, lectures.   I. Title.
BS534.5.A45   1984   220.6'01   83-19935
ISBN 0-8170-1002-5

The name JUDSON PRESS is registered as a trademark in the U.S. Patent Office.
Printed in the U.S.A. ⊕

For
CANAAN
Child of Our Flesh
Whose Name Embodies Our Hope
That the Whole Human Family Can Live in a
Land Flowing with Milk and Honey

Contents

Preface

This book develops ways in which the historical-critical interpretation of Scripture can be a servant of preaching. While I am not the first to offer suggestions in this regard, I hope the present work will encourage preaching to come to live birth as well as make a modest contribution to the flow of traffic between the academy and the parish.

Strictly speaking, many of the exegetical disciplines are descriptive and not theological. They intend to account for the formation of texts on the basis of empirical evidence to the extent that some aspects of contemporary biblical interpretation are accused of reductionism. Indeed, some scholars do seem to reduce the formation and meaning of biblical texts to the interaction of observable phenomena, such as sociologically predictable patterns of behavior.

While theological neutrality may be important to certain exercises of the historical-critical method, one of the specific aims of preaching is to make a theological claim. Perhaps, then, we can see that empirical observation and description can provide data for theological reflection. For instance, if Norman Gottwald is correct in his reconstruction of the "Conquest" as a revolutionary uprising of already established residents, that reconstruction does not fully account for the theological interpretation of the phenomena, which is that the Lord ". . . brought us into this place and gave us this land . . ." (Deuteronomy 26:9).[1] The fact that a text can be interpreted sociologically (or structurally or psychologically or redaction-critically) does not exhaust the meaning of the text.

As a supplement to each chapter, suggestions for further reading are given. These suggestions are intended only to be representative avenues through which one might enter the larger discussions. Insofar as possible, I have tried to list volumes that are still in print.

For the most part, my secondary research base has been limited deliberately to materials which a pastor could reasonably own. This should reinforce the notion that one need not read German or live next door to a major theological library in order to conduct a serious and creative study of a Bible passage. Indeed, while I join the biblical guild in advocating historical criticism as the most responsible approach to a biblical text, that method is no substitute for one's own analysis of and response to the text.

These themes first stirred in my consciousness while I was co-pastor, with my spouse, of the First Christian Church, Grand Island, Nebraska. They first came to public expression as one of the Edwin E. Voigt Memorial Lectures on Preaching (1981), given under the auspices of the Southern and Central Illinois Conferences of the United Methodist Church at McKendree College, Lebanon, Illinois. I take this opportunity to express my appreciation to the lectureship committee and to its chair, Dr. Steven N. Perrin, for the kind invitation to bring the lectures and to the pastors and spouses whose gracious response relieved the anxiety of one who stood on lecture legs for the first time.

The full text was developed during a wonderful year as Lilly Visiting Professor at Christian Theological Seminary, Indianapolis. I am honored to be part of that community and to be identified with its vision for the ministry of the whole church.

I am especially grateful to the members of the library staff who were attentive to my bibliographical needs while our personal library was stored in a bunker at the Cornhusker Munitions Plant, Hall County, Nebraska, while we sojourned our first year in Indiana. During World War II and the Vietnam war, the bunker held thousand-pound bombs prior to their shipment to the battlefields. After our books, along with our household goods, had been set in place and we were ready to lock the door and to leave for Indianapolis, my spouse set one of our peace books on top of the stack. That is not a bad picture of ministry today.

Ronald J. Allen

Christian Theological Seminary
Indianapolis
The Festival of the Resurrection, 1983

1

The Changing Situation in Sermon Preparation

Our habits of preparing to preach often limit what we find in the biblical text. Sometimes our preparation time is battered and emaciated, as if under a meat mallet. At other times, when we can catch a few sheltered moments for study, we are not always able to get the maximum benefit for the effort expended.

Think of what is, for many, a typical Monday morning. The desk is barely recognizable beneath a pile of messages left on Sunday. The church paper needs to be published and the secretary (who is more mechanic than poet) must get every semicolon right. One of the elders drops by to ramble about the declining Sunday church school situation and about how "we had more kids than we knew what to do with when we were down in the old church." And the phone rings. And rings. And rings.

Toward the end of the morning when the secretary asks for a sermon title (to be printed in the church paper), we open the lectionary and, without meaning to exploit the text, look for a theme that says "preach me." Or we rummage around in the Bible (or sermon file) hoping to find something that will speak, however quietly, to our imaginations.

The week that looked like a gigantic, open park on Monday is

soon crowded with potholes and briars—making pastoral calls, filling
in the details the sponsor should have taken care of in preparation
for the youth group trip, soothing a parishioner's hurt feelings because the birth announcement of her great-niece in Pittsfield, Maine,
was omitted from the worship service, accepting another responsibility with the local draft counseling network, dealing with the death
of a longtime member in a nursing home. Such things can easily
combine to push sermon preparation toward the end of the week.

All of a sudden it is Thursday morning, or afternoon, or Friday
morning . . . or later. The notepaper is still bare. So we take down
that old friend *The Interpreter's Bible* and look at it—not so much
at the text at the top of the page and not so much at the exegesis
on the middle of the page, but at the homiletical help at the bottom.
We turn to William Barclay's *Daily Study Bible Series* and notice
that the three or four points he makes in his discussion of the text
would make a fine outline for a sermon.

We take the text, fresh and yeasty like a ball of dough, and put
it under the rolling pin of our systematic theology (usually worked
out in seminary days) and flatten the text into the shape of a favorite
theological theme—the love of God, the surprise of God, the judgment of God (and our anger) at middle-class North American Christians.

Sunday morning comes. We gather up what we have, tie it together
with a few illustrations out of the Saturday paper, perhaps a joke
from AAUW or Kiwanis, and throw it out like a lifeline. We hope
the knots will hold until someone who grabs on can get close enough
to shore for us to reach them by the hand of counseling or political
action.

Even for the disciplined, who set aside regular preparation time,
the well sometimes runs dry and the imagination is left to pump
with little to draw upon. How often I have left the pulpit feeling as
if I were onto something, near a breakthrough that never came.

In addition to complex cultural and theological issues, it seems
to me that three practical factors frustrate preparation for preaching.
First is the press of contemporary parish life. Second is biblical
illiteracy. Third is an exegetical model which is more at home in
the Society of Biblical Literature than in the local church.

The Press of Parish Life

Over the past thirty years the perception of the place of the minister in parish life has changed. Thirty years ago the model of the minister was the resident theologian, the scholar-pastor whose primary work was to reflect on the meaning of life in the light of Scripture and theology. Then came the 1960s, the activist years. In the 1970s managerial concepts from the corporate world were grafted onto the life of the church so that today the minister is as much manager as theologian or activist. We even speak of "MBO" (ministry by objective), an adaptation of industry's "management by objective."

In addition, the rapid expansion of the need for particular ministerial skills has been observed in the last fifteen years. Ever more sophisticated educational experiences prepare the pastor for such diverse ministries as intensive individual counseling, growth-group leadership, divorce recovery workshops, premarital guidance, special time with the terminally ill. As the average age of the membership of the main-line Protestant denominations advances, we spend more and more time in senior citizen facilities. A socially aware pastor is involved in community issues and is often on the front line witnessing for human rights, peace, or a similar issue of the hour. The first paragraph of any manual on church growth will make it clear that the pastor is *the key person* in church growth.

Harry Emerson Fosdick is remembered as having spent an hour in the study for every minute in the pulpit. Does any pastor today have the luxury of twenty hours behind a locked door? Especially in situations with only one professional staff member, important dimensions of parish life would soon suffer, if not diminish altogether.

Biblical Illiteracy

Among main-line laity and clergy, biblical illiteracy is no longer unusual. By biblical illiteracy I mean a lack of familiarity with the content of the Scriptures as well as uncertainty about how to interpret them. The problem is of both method and meaning.

On one level, many of us do not know basic facts of the biblical stories. Who were the Moabites? Are they different from the Canaanites? Who lived first, Elisha or Isaiah? Where do we find the genealogy of Jesus? Of course, facts do not make righteousness, but if we do not know the stories, how can we live out of them?

On another level, we are not always sure of the meaning of biblical texts or what, if anything, they have to do with us. A serious problem is that many main-line pastors lack the skill to use the critical methodology of biblical interpretation and, more important, do not fully understand the significance of its results for preaching. William Barclay's comments can be transported directly from the study to the pulpit in nearly the same amount of time it takes to read a page of a Hermeneia commentary.

In seminary, of course, ministerial students are introduced to basic principles of biblical interpretation. In some schools, content exams are still required, but the content of the Hebrew Bible can scarcely become a part of one's bones in sixteen hurried weeks.[1] The introductory courses tend to focus on the fundamental questions of the documents. Who wrote them? When? To whom? From where? In what situations? In order to graduate with a degree in ministry a student will ordinarily demonstrate competence in exegetical method.

But once in the parish, the pertinence of form criticism, redaction criticism, and the newer critical disciplines (whose names may never even cross a pastor's desk) fades under the pressure of funerals, hospital calls, weddings, the financial drive, and the CROP walk. We are introduced in seminary to an academic model with a fair amount of jargon and German and sent to live in a world in which the leader of the congregation thinks *Geschichte* is an electric razor.

Exegetical Method

The manner in which most students in main-line seminaries are trained to do exegesis is frequently more at home in the Society of Biblical Literature than in the church. Most of us were trained to interpret the Bible for preaching in the same way that we would write an article for the *Journal of Biblical Literature*.

The problem is not with the historical-critical method per se but with our application of it to preaching and teaching. While the historical-critical method has been liberating in our understanding of the text, especially in leading us away from some of the dead ends of fundamentalism (even while creating some cul-de-sacs of its own), it is too cumbersome to be used full-blown on a weekly basis in the parish.

The method itself can be outlined quickly. After selecting a text and determining its meaningful limits, we practice textual criticism, that is, we establish the most likely wording of the text in the original language on the basis of external (primarily manuscript) and internal criteria. With lexicon in hand, we make a formal translation, noting important matters of grammar. At some point we ask the fundamental questions (who wrote it? and the like) and take account of the literary context in which it is found. With Bible atlases, dictionaries, geographies, and histories we try to construct a picture of the historical background in which the text was born.

The form of the text is identified as well as the function of the form in the ancient world. Philology (word studies) is a point at which the traditional model has proved consistently informative for preaching. Frequently word studies are directly useful in preaching in a way that establishing the authorship of Esther may not be. And so much the better if one of the words has a hidden meaning, some ancient nuance that may cause false teeth to drop. The concordance awakens us to how the word is used elsewhere and alerts us to correlative themes.

In redaction criticism the development of the text is traced from its original setting through the various forms in which it circulated prior to being woven into its present literary context and finally to its present placement and use. Redaction criticism is the latest discipline of biblical criticism with which pastors who completed seminary prior to 1970 may be familiar.

At the end, we are asked to make a theological assessment of the importance of the passage. Called hermeneutics, the task is to find contemporary meaning in the ancient text. At least a fair number of biblical scholars identify a reason for their work as strengthening the life of the church. In published works, few address the hermeneutical question directly; and those who attempt to relate their work to preaching frequently do so by way of a small chapter tacked onto the end of a major work, thereby reinforcing the notion that preaching is the streamer of theology and biblical studies.[2] Thus, I think my teachers were right: "More exegesis fails at the point of a statement of its relevance than anywhere else."[3]

In seminary, when we have accumulated a respectable number of index cards, we shuffle them, write the paper according to the guidelines of Kate Turabian, the MLA style sheet, or one of the newer (but no less stylized) formats. Douglas Stuart describes the disparity between the exegetical expectation in theological school and in the parish.

> The term paper necessitates substantial research and writing, is in many ways narrow and technical, and involves the writer in the production of a formal, typed manuscript to be evaluated by a single professor, with special attention to methodological competence and comprehensiveness, including notes and bibliography. The sermon is usually composed in ten hours or less (total), must avoid being excessively narrow or technical, does not require a formal manuscript, is evaluated by a large and diverse group of listeners who are mostly not scholars and who are less interested in methodological competence than in the practical results thereof.[4]

Now, I do not wish to be misunderstood. The traditional exercise of the historical-critical method is important to the questions of the guild of biblical scholars. Its insights are, indeed, critical for preaching. However, in its traditional form it is too cumbersome—and often too lacking in apparent significance—to be used weekly.

What do we need? To go back to another time when pastoral life was simpler? To use predigested materials? To resonate with the text, letting it vibrate our imaginations into activity? To do so would be to turn away from the controls, gains, and insights of historical-critical research.

We need an approach to exegesis, which is the servant of the work of preaching. We need a disciplined, informed approach that utilizes the insights of critical exegesis and is simple enough to be practiced on a weekly basis. Toward this end several of the major exegetical disciplines are examined from the standpoint of their contributions to preaching.

Ask the Key Questions

In the following chapters I try to express some of the fundamental issues of the major disciplines in the form of questions we can ask of the text. While the questions arise from the critical disciplines, I believe they are appropriate for the life of a parish.

An important corollary is that the same questions that are asked of the text may also be asked of the commentaries and exegetical resources. One reason we do not receive more help in sermon preparation from the secondary resources (especially the more academic ones) is that we do not ask provocative questions of them. They may contain insights which may be illuminating but which are hidden in the dust of the academic apparatus.

The questions are not intended to be an end in themselves. Indeed, there is a sense in which we are limited by the size and number of the questions we ask. Instead, they are intended to be starting points. I hope they will provide that moment when the miner, deep in the earth, strikes the wall with a pick and in the damp lamplight sees the glint of ore.

While the methodologies are considered individually, exegesis is integrated and holistic. Many of the disciplines are related to one another as parent to child. Therefore, one may wish to use the questions in a "walk-around" way, that is, walk around and into the theater of the text, looking at it from the different perspectives of the disciplines and then climbing to the balcony for an overview.

After chapter 2, which deals with introductory matters, each chapter deals with one discipline. In parallel form, each chapter discusses the pertinence of that discipline to preaching, formulates key questions from its viewpoint, illustrates with a case study how that discipline may inform preaching, and offers suggestions for further reading. The disciplines discussed include examination of the historical background, philology, form criticism, redaction criticism, structuralism, sociological exegesis, liberation exegesis, interpretation of a biblical text as a work of art, canonical criticism, and hermeneutics.[5]

Suggestions for Further Reading

The exegetical disciplines, their practice and interrelationship, are explained in a number of useful works. Basic introductions which combine thoroughness with economy of size are found in the series *Guides to Biblical Scholarship* published by Fortress Press. Brief explanations are found in *The Interpreter's Dictionary of the Bible,* ed. George A. Buttrick (Nashville: Abingdon Press, 1964) and especially in *The Interpreter's Dictionary of the Bible, Supplementary Volume,* ed. Keith R. Crim, *et al.* (1976) in which one should especially see L. E. Keck and G. M. Tucker, "Exegesis," pp. 296–303. Basic information is given in compact, dictionary-like form in Richard N. Soulen, *Handbook of Biblical Criticism,* rev. ed. (Atlanta: John Knox Press, 1981) and Nicholas Turner, *Handbook for Biblical Studies* (Philadelphia: The Westminster Press, 1982).

Among the useful systematic presentations of exegetical process are Otto Kaiser and Werner G. Kummel, *Exegetical Method: A Student Handbook,* rev. ed., trans. E. V. Goetschius and M. J. O'Connell (New York: The Seabury Press, Inc., 1981); William D. Thompson, *Preaching Biblically: Exegesis and Interpretation* (Nashville: Abingdon Press, 1981); Reginald H. Fuller, *The Use of the Bible in Preaching* (Philadelphia: Fortress Press, 1981); Douglas Stuart, *Old Testament Exegesis: A Primer for Students and Pastors* (Philadelphia: The Westminster Press, 1980); and John Hayes and Carl Holladay, *A Beginner's Handbook for Biblical Exegesis* (Atlanta: John Knox Press, 1982). A provocative but controversial approach to biblical interpretation is Walter Wink, *The Bible in Human Transformation: Towards a New Paradigm for Biblical Study* (Philadelphia: Fortress Press, 1980) and *Transforming Bible Study: A Leader's Guide* (Nashville: Abingdon Press, 1980). Of interest to students of the New Testament is Patrick Henry, *New Directions in New Testament Study* (Philadelphia: The Westminster Press, 1979).

2

Opening the Door to the World of the Text

When a pastor settles down with a text to begin sermon preparation, he or she is seldom a tabula rasa, a blank slate, on which the text can write its message in clear, bold letters. As I begin sermon preparation, I click my tongue over the breakfast cereal still caught between my teeth and remember the noisy issues of the morning news, the embarrassment of almost falling asleep in the warm home of a shut-in, the cabaret of feelings evoked by a recent wedding, unbalanced checkbooks at home and church, the need to find someone to be chairperson of the evangelism committee, the local hassles created by the latest pronouncement of the World Council of Churches and the grisly report of what we civilly call "violations of human rights." In just a few days, I will again step to the pulpit. The people expect to hear a fresh, living, even powerful word, and God knows I want to bring them one.

When kept under control by responsible exegesis and theology, such factors can make me sensitive to dimensions of the text I might otherwise pass by on the other side. While I hope they will be a life-giving part of my relationship with the text, I am aware that that relationship could end in stillbirth because of their inappropriate intrusion.

To sermon preparation I may also bring presuppositions about the meaning of the text. If the text is familiar, especially if I have worked with it before, I may short-circuit exegesis by assuming that my memories, prior acquaintance, and even intuition are sufficient preparation for preaching from that text; for example, Hebrews 11, the faith chapter.

We may thereby assume more familiarity with the text than we actually have. Because at funerals I often hear (and use) the famous words "In my Father's house are many rooms . . .," I may uncritically limit the use of that text to the occasion of death. The parable of the talents can easily become a charter of capitalism, a concern quite foreign to first-century listeners. In my zeal to beef up attendance at the Sunday service, I may invoke the Fourth Commandment with a voice reminiscent of the thunder at Mount Sinai, thus overlooking the actual content of Exodus 20:8-11 in which the purpose of the sabbath is to provide a day of rest, and that on the seventh day.

A familiar text is sometimes like a visit with an old cousin: we may not expect to learn much that is new, exciting, or challenging. In fact, as I think about my early experiences of weekly sermon preparation, I am embarrassed to remember the number of times that I did not even read the text before sinking my shovel into the soil to prepare the foundation of the sermon.

While we cannot erase the concerns of our hearts and minds or our presuppositions about the meaning of the text, we do not want them to predetermine our conversation (or confrontation) with the text. Instead, we consciously want to meet the text on its own terms. This involves our expectation as we approach the text as well as some practical ways of beginning.

A Basic Expectation: The Bible As Strange World

In exegesis, as in life, expectation plays an important role in fulfillment. What we expect is usually what we find. If we think of the text as old and tired, we may not even notice the stagnant air which has settled in the study. The sermon of a pastor with this attitude can provide little more than a few comforting words, a benign pat on the arm, perhaps a lump in the throat, and some nagging reminders.

One of the gains of the historical-critical method is to increase our sense of expectation. Indeed, in the words of Karl Barth, we can expect to find a strange new world within the Bible.[1]

On one level the strangeness of the Bible is related to its cultural context. When we lift our eyes up to the hills, we do not see Canaanite fertility altars. Idioms in Hebrew and Greek, once as sharp and piercing as arrows readied for battle, are now crusted over and dull. The Western scientific way of thinking, which governs much of contemporary biblical interpretation, is as foreign to the oriental mind as the Cadillac is to the camel.

On another level, the strangeness of the Bible is related to our values and to the way in which the North American culture has co-opted the Bible as a source of blessing on our values, economic and political system, and life-style. Because of civil religion as well as the almost unconscious human predilection to identify with heroes and winners, we have tended to regard the Bible as a word of confirmation of our way of life. In the United States it is easy to think of God as middle-class and the Bible as a kind of handbook for better family relationships. However, as often as not, the Bible asks us to look at life from strange and different perspectives. Blessing comes to a sheik and his spouse in the form of a lifetime sojourn. The Lord of Hosts is the God of peace. Wealth is found not at the savings and loan but in faithful stewardship. God is free to justify even the ungodly.

Of course, we cannot satisfactorily regard the Bible as a market-place of Sunday surprises. How often can a congregation be surprised when surprise becomes the weekly fare? We can, however, begin sermon preparation with the basic expectation that the text may be something other than a divine stamp of "prime" on the meat of our existence.

Ironically we may discover with Fred Craddock that by establishing a certain distance from the text, we are able to be engaged more deeply by it.[2] A sense of distance may prevent us from prematurely pulling the draperies on the windows through which the light of the text may enter. When our defenses are down, the text can more easily do its business with us.

From Expectation to Exegesis

Before giving the text detailed attention—in fact before reading it closely or sharpening a pencil in preparation for close work—it is often helpful to jot down the first associations that the text calls to mind. Sometimes these associations take the form of questions. Sometimes the text sparks an idea whose dimensions are only slightly less than an atomic reaction, while sometimes it stirs a thought as muted as the sound of the neighbor girl's flute drifting across the backyard. Frequently I remember earlier associations with the text— a sermon, my childhood Sunday church school classmates gathered around a flannelgraph, a vicious seminary discussion in which the stakes were high. A real-life experience or a scene from a movie or novel may come spontaneously to mind. I am not afraid to follow the text down heretofore unnoticed avenues, to traverse alleyways about which I should have better taste, to let the text take its own path through the roadways of the mind.

This process cannot be forced too much or it may break down at an inopportune time. In the process I may discover that I do not come to the text naively and that I have a rather full-bodied pre-understanding. When the pre-understanding is outlined, I can place it in dialogue with the developing exegesis and sermon.

To be sure that I am dealing with a meaningful unit of thought, I mark the limits of the passage. I like to make my own translation, but because of the large number of excellent translations already available in English, I do not feel guilty when I am unable to do so. I do try to read several different Bible versions, particularly the Revised Standard Version, *The Jerusalem Bible*, Today's English Version, the New International Version, and *The New English Bible*. Using different versions allows me to sense how other interpreters have felt the stress, emphasis, and movement of the passage.[3] As the exegesis deepens, I will compare the translators' emphases with my own. Although I do not rely on it for serious work or for the public reading of the Scriptures, I do look at *The Living Bible* because it is so widely used by members of many congregations.

Making my own outline helps me to unravel knotted strands of thought like the single sentences in Paul that are six, eight, or ten verses in length. Sometimes I make my own paraphrase, trying to express the thrust of the passage in vivid, graphic images drawn from the life of my own community (rather like Clarence Jordan has done in his Cotton Patch translation of parts of the New Testament into the idiom of rural Georgia). Often I am unable to do this until the exegesis is complete, and sometimes it becomes a part of the sermon itself.

Frequently I walk down the hallway to the empty sanctuary and read the text aloud with feeling, inflection, pauses, and attention to volume and timing. This causes my mind to slow down and ponder words and expressions—especially unfamiliar ones—which I might ordinarily gloss over.

Much of the Bible has a long oral history. Before it was put into written form, and even after, much of the Bible was intended for the ear and the mouth (to be heard, spoken, or sung) rather than for the eye (to be read). Reading aloud, therefore, may set in motion intuitive sympathy with the text. If done with expression, consonant with the tone of the text, it may call to consciousness some of the feelings that would have been evoked by the text in its original setting.

I read the text aloud several times, each time with a different emphasis, pace, and stress, so that I can imagine different ways in which the words might have been spoken and heard. The inflection and tone of the voice can make a significant difference in the way a text is interpreted. Consider the differences in feeling and in meaning when the climax of the poem of Job is read in these ways: with a sense of awe and majesty, like a trial lawyer's question, and with the exasperation of a mother whose child has just meandered home an hour late for supper.

> "Where were you when I laid the foundation of the
>   earth?
> Tell me, if you have understanding.
> Who determined its measurements—surely you
> know!"
>   —Job 38:4-5

Of course I cannot determine the inflection with which to read the text in the service of worship until the exegesis has opened its meaning. But reading the text in several different intonations may awaken me to possible meanings I might otherwise overlook. Careful exegesis can confirm or deny the validity of those meanings.

In addition, I try to read and hear the text from different viewpoints. The saga of Joseph is quite different when read first from the viewpoint of Joseph, next from the point of view of the brothers, and even more different when heard from the perspective of an Egyptian. The message of Micah elicits one reaction when I hear it as a member of the ruling class and quite another reaction when I hear it from the position of a peasant whose land has been taken away. The epistles, in particular, were intended to be read publicly in congregational meetings. On occasion I have been helped by making a tape recording of the text and listening to the tape as if I were sitting in a house church. Again, the exegesis will determine the most fitting emphases for public reading, but hearing and reading the text from different perspectives can open doors that might otherwise remain closed.

An important corollary results for the service of worship: In the public reading, the Scriptures will come alive. In many services of worship, the reading of the lessons from Scripture is as flat as a popped balloon, as if neither the reader nor the listener expects to hear any news at all, much less Good News. "ListenforthewordofGod . . . MayGodaddtoourunderstandingthisreadingandtoGod'snamebe gloryandpraise."

As a part of preparation for Sunday, I want to prepare myself to read the text with the tempo, volume, pauses, commas, exclamation points, paragraphs, and accents appropriate to the discoveries made in the course of exegesis. If the text is an alleluia, I want the people to feel it rise up within themselves. If the text is a story, I want the people to participate in it; I want the reading to stimulate their emotions and set in motion the rhythms that characterize actual events.[4]

Of course the tone of the reading should complement that of the sermon. While the oral reading of the Bible is no substitute for seasoned interpretation, a well-read passage can arouse the congregation to its hunger for that word which is ". . . living and active, sharper than any two-edged sword, piercing to the division of soul and spirit, of joints and marrow . . ." (Hebrews 4:12).[5]

Suggestions for Further Reading

The expectation with which we approach the Bible embraces topics as diverse as biblical inspiration and the relationship of faith and culture. I list here some references which outline major issues. R. M. Grant, *A Short History of Biblical Interpretation* (New York: Macmillan, Inc., 1963); Paul J. Achtemeier, *The Inspiration of Scripture: Problems and Proposals* (Philadelphia: The Westminster Press, 1980); William Countryman, *Biblical Authority or Biblical Tyranny? Scripture and the Christian Pilgrimage* (Philadelphia: Fortress Press, 1982); Phyllis Bird, *The Bible as the Church's Book* (Philadelphia: The Westminster Press, 1982); Raymond E. Brown, *The Critical Meaning of the Bible* (New York: Paulist Press, 1981); James Barr, *The Bible in the Modern World* (New York: Oxford University Press, Inc., 1981) and *The Scope and Authority of the Bible* (Philadelphia: The Westminster Press, 1981); Bernhard W. Anderson, *The Living Word of the Bible* (Philadelphia: The Westminster Press, 1979); James D. Smart, *The Strange Silence of the Bible in the Church: A Study in Hermeneutics* (Philadelphia: The Westminster Press, 1970); Paul D. Hanson, *The Diversity of Scripture* (Philadelphia: Fortress Press, 1982); Peter Stuhlmacher, *Historical Criticism and Theological Interpretation of Scripture,* trans. Roy Harrisville (Philadelphia: Fortress Press, 1977); *Conflicting Ways of Interpreting the Bible,* ed. Hans Kung and Jurgen Moltmann (New York: The Seabury Press, Inc., 1980); and Ferdinand Hahn, *Historical Investigation and New Testament Faith,* trans. Robert Maddox (Philadelphia: Fortress Press, 1983).

With practice and discipline anyone can become an effective oral interpreter of the Bible. A basic work is Charlotte E. Lee, *Oral Reading of the Scriptures* (Boston: Houghton Mifflin Co., 1964). Related but more general works are Harold A. Brack, *Effective Oral Interpretation for Religious Leaders* (Englewood Cliffs: Prentice-

Hall Inc., 1964) and Charlotte I. Lee, *Oral Interpretation*, rev. ed. (Boston: Houghton Mifflin Co., 1971). Still valuable is Dwight E. Stevenson and Charles F. Diehl, *Reaching People from the Pulpit, a Guide to Effective Sermon Delivery* (Grand Rapids: Baker Book House, 1970), which contains exercises for increasing the quality and variety of the speaking voice.

3

The Historical Background

In the broad sense, much of biblical exegesis is concerned with recovering the historical background of the text. Knowledge of that background often allows us to see ancient dimensions of meaning which are not obvious to the modern eye.

Other chapters will focus on special aspects of the historical background such as sociological phenomena. This chapter speaks more generally of the importance of knowing "what was happening" in the historical situation in which the text came to life, especially the mood and situation of the people to whom the text was addressed. It follows that our interpretation will sometimes be heightened if we understand the situation described within the text itself.

To communicate the full force of a text in preaching, we may want to create in our listeners something of the mood and feeling that was present in the context(s) to which the text was earlier addressed. A word, like a seed, is intended for a certain type of soil, and sometimes we need to prepare the listening soil. A decision as to the importance of creating such soil in the course of the sermon can be made only after spading up the historical background.

The Historical Setting to Which the Text Was Spoken

Traditionally the approach to determining the historical setting of a text has been "introductory questions":
1. Who was the author?
2. Where was the text written?
3. When was it written?
4. What was the situation for which it was written?
5. Why (for what purpose) was it written?

The secondary sources will often be of as much direct help as the text itself in answering such questions.[1]

While the preacher ought to ask all five questions of every text, generally speaking, for sermon preparation the last two will be of greater help than the first three. In many cases we have no access to the name, much less to the personality, of the author of a pericope. Around the camp fire, who first told the tales now embedded in the Pentateuch? We can no longer identify the first singers of the Psalms or the tellers of the miracle stories. It is equally difficult to speculate about the personality of biblical characters in our peculiarly modern way, as when we refer to Jeremiah as "the weeping prophet" or to Paul as the "abrasive apostle."

Further, except in special circumstances, few preachers will want to rehearse something like the source theory of the Synoptic Gospels before the congregation. The authorship of Ephesians is an important issue in tracing the development of early Christianity but will not regularly be a critical fulcrum on which the sermon itself is pushed.

Much the same is true of the date and place of writing. Indeed, these cannot always be fixed with certainty; and even when they can, that information is not likely to flow directly to the pulpit. The fact that the Book of Daniel was written about 165 B.C.E. or that Paul wrote his first letter to the Corinthians at Ephesus will, in and of itself, add little to the homiletical storehouse.

From the viewpoint of sermon preparation, the historical background is most important for "getting a feel" for the world in which the text came to life and to which it spoke. A clear grasp of issues, events, and feelings alive at that time will help us understand what is and what is not at stake in a given text.

Consider some examples. The authentic prophecies of Micah (roughly chapters 1–3) were spoken against the backdrop of corruption and collapse in the Southern Kingdom. Political and religious leaders had combined to exploit the lower classes, particularly the rural farmers. The religious establishment—which should have been aware of the demand of God for justice in all arenas of life—not only tolerated these conditions but also blessed them. From the viewpoint of the rural poor, Micah preached judgment on the political, economic, and religious establishment: God will make Zion as a plowed field. In the sermon the preacher may want to create a sense of the feelings and issues associated with those conditions.

The stories of the Book of Daniel take on fresh perspective when read through the eyes of a faithful Jew, perhaps hiding in a cave in the mountains, about the time of the Maccabean revolt. Jewish life and culture had been systematically compromised and sold out to the Gentile forces of occupation, much to the disgust of faithful Jews. The last straw was the attempt to negate Jewish religion by erecting an altar to Zeus in the temple at Jerusalem and by erecting similar altars in the countryside. Jews were ordered to worship at these altars and to eat swine. Against this backdrop a tale of three young men who pass unscathed through the fiery furnace is no bedtime story. Such stories encouraged the faithful population to keep the Covenant despite the presence of Gentile troops whose purpose was to force obedience by the sword. In the sermon, the preacher may want to create a sense of that revolutionary time.

Recent research indicates that as part of the background out of which the Fourth Gospel came, there was intense conflict between the synagogue and the church. Members of the church for which John wrote may have been Jewish Christians who were forcibly excluded from the synagogue, perhaps by use of the famous benediction in which God was asked to curse the heretics, commonly interpreted to be Christians. In the Gospel of John the phrase "the Jews" is not intended to recall persons alive at the time of Jesus as much as it is a dramatic device to represent figures who opposed the church in John's time.

Against this background, the healing of the man born blind (John

9) takes on meaning beyond that of a miracle story. The treatment
of the beggar at the hands of Jewish authorities may represent the
treatment of the church at the hands of the synagogue. We should
be careful not to use the text as a basis, however subtle, for anti-
Semitism. The words of Jesus in John 9:35–41 thus take on a deep
existential import. In the course of the sermon, the preacher may
want to create the feelings associated with being excluded as a
context for hearing the story of the healing and the ensuing dialogue.

We typically hear Paul's hymn on love (1 Corinthians 13) in the
tender atmosphere of a wedding service. The words, in fact, are at
the center of Paul's discussion of the life of a congregation deeply
troubled by spiritual enthusiasm (1 Corinthians 12–14). That is
somewhat foreign to the average main-line congregation which is
hardly beset with the problem of overenthusiasm in worship. Yet,
against the backdrop of the supercharged worship life of the Corinthian congregation, as well as the general breakdown of relationships
in that congregation, 1 Corinthians 13 is read with real strength and
what I would call "guts." In the sermon the preacher may want the
congregation to be sensitive to the division, confusion, and rancor
of the situation to which these words were addressed.

We need also to remember that some parts of texts were directed
to more than one setting. As we have them they were spoken (or
written) according to the situation of the final canonical author.
Many texts were also addressed earlier to radically different situations and were reshaped by subsequent authors and editors in response to the needs of their own times.

For example, we can trace at least three layers of tradition in the
story of the conquest of Jericho (Joshua 6). It was given its final
form by the Deuteronomic historian for his or her situation, a time
of confusion in which people were straying from the Covenant.
"Why has God let economic, political, and spiritual collapse happen
to us?" The story of the conquest of Jericho, pictured as a mighty
fortified city, illustrates the basic principle underlying Deuteronomic
theology: if the people of the Deuteronomist's day, like Joshua, will
do what God commands, then God will bless them, as Joshua was
blessed, with victory. An earlier generation may have used the story

to give credence to a liturgical procession which celebrated the fact that God keeps promises regardless of human merit. At the time of the actual conquest, Jericho was probably little more than a village of huts which was overrun by Hebrews.[2]

Each of these layers will yield a different sermon. Preachers need to be aware of the different situations to which a given text was addressed so that they may decide consciously which situation will inform the sermon.

The Situation Described in a Text

In addition, some texts make reference to particular physical settings, for example, geography or architecture, or to a particular life setting such as a battle or the cult. Occasionally it will help us enter the world of the text if we can make appropriate sensory associations with the setting. The idea is not to imagine we are Philistines on the plain of Jezreel, but to gain a sensory, emotive appreciation of the text. Physical, geographical, and even sensory associations can sometimes contribute to theological reference.

The five senses are an important grid through which to run the text.

1. What would I see in this text?
   E.g., what would I see from the top of Mount Carmel (1 Kings 18)?
2. What would I hear in this text?
   E.g., what would I hear in Psalm 150?
3. What would I smell in this text?
   E.g., what would I smell in the story of Zechariah going to the temple (Luke 1)?
4. What would I touch in this text?
   E.g., what would I touch if I were the woman with the twelve-year hemorrhage who touched the hem of Jesus' garment (Mark 5)?
5. What would I taste in this text?
   What would I taste at the Last Supper (Matthew 26)?

In the case of some texts, these questions will yield little of value for interpretation.

In particular, prophets and poets speak and write using careful,

sensory imagery. A rudimentary exegetical responsibility is to identify the references of the imagery and, thus, what sensations the
imagery might evoke in the hearers.

Zephaniah, for instance, describes the day of the Lord.

"A cry will be heard from the Fish Gate,
a wail from the Second Quarter,
a loud crash from the hills."

—Zephaniah 1:10

The prophet speaks in specific images. In context the cumulative
effect of such images is a picture of the whole population in profound
sorrow because of its destruction. In order to project the full force
of the prophetic message, the preacher could involve himself or
herself to the extent that a similar sorrow is evoked within the
congregation.

Amos speaks of a famine of ". . . hearing the words of the
LORD"(Amos 8:11). Congregations that feel that famine are likely
to be good seedbeds for the text.

Other types of texts, as well, stimulate the sensory faculties.
While the ability to visualize, smell, or feel a scene may not have
a theological import, it helps the scene come alive. Elijah's plight
becomes more poignant when we can picture him under the broom
tree. The full effect of a battle looms larger when we can imagine
its setting, feel the savage impact of sword against flesh, hear the
cries of the dying, and smell the rotting flesh. When we feel hunger,
we can better understand why David ate the sacred bread from the
altar.

Occasionally we find an intrinsic connection between a sensory
experience referred to in a text and the meaning of the text. In
Romans 6, Paul describes baptism as dying and rising with Christ.
In baptismal practice, the candidate enters the water, is submerged,
and emerges. To enter the depth of the text, it is important to feel
the water covering the self and then to feel the emergence of the
self. In the water we are symbolically entombed, but when we rise
from the water, it is as if we have risen to a new life.

Indeed, the experience of immersion is integral to the meaning
of baptism because the rite itself speaks to us at the deepest levels

of consciousness. Rites of water initiation touch taproots that extend to the dawn of human consciousness. The meaning of baptism cannot be compressed into a single theological statement, but a part of its meaning is communicated through the experience itself.[3]

Paul uses the motif of baptism to serve his larger theological purposes. He can do so because he can take for granted the common experience of baptism shared by the recipients of the letter.

Neither a sermon nor a biblical text is a stand-in for baptism itself. However, the preacher's description can be vivid enough that the people in the congregation can imaginatively feel the water covering them and then feel themselves rising to walk in the newness of life in the new age. Recollecting the experience, of course, will not substitute for theological analysis of the meaning of baptism, but it will enrich significantly the homiletical experience.

Key Questions

There are six key questions that will help us to understand the situation to which the text was addressed and the situation described by the text.

1. What level of the history of the text will inform the sermon?
2. The introductory questions:
   a. Who was the author of the text?
   b. Where was the text written?
   c. When was the text written?
   d. What was the situation for which the text was written?
   e. Why (for what purpose) was the text written?
3. What would it feel like to be in that situation?
4. Is it important for the congregation to experience something of the atmosphere and feeling of that situation in order to be receptive to the full force of the text?
5. When I read this text, what do I:
   a. See?
   b. Hear?
   c. Smell?
   d. Touch?
   e. Taste?
6. Is it important for the congregation to experience imaginatively

any of these in order to feel the full force of the text?

If the preacher concludes that it is important for the congregation to experience some aspect of the world of the text, he or she will have to create a vehicle for so doing. One approach might be to describe the world of the text in vivid language. Another might be to use contemporary images and stories to evoke the same awareness and feelings experienced by the characters in the ancient setting.

Case Study: Isaiah 40:1-11

1. What level of the history of the text will inform the sermon? Commentators note that this text was addressed to at least two different situations. The more recent, in its canonical form, was to the community which had returned from the Exile and attempted to reestablish the Jewish homeland. The prior setting was the Exile itself and it is that level on which this case study is based.

2. The introductory questions.

a. Who was the author of the text? While the author is commonly called Second Isaiah, we know neither the actual name nor his or her personality. The same author wrote chapters 40–55.

b. Where was the text written? Babylonia.

c. When was the text written? The text appears to have been written about 540 B.C.E. Certainly it was composed around the time that Cyrus attacked Babylonia.

d. What was the situation for which the text was written? The text is addressed to a community of Jews, in exile in Babylonia, who longed for their homeland. Jerusalem was in ruins and the social institutions of Judaism had collapsed. The exiles were the second generation to be separated from the most important symbols of Jewish religion and identity, particularly the temple. The world political situation was unstable. The people were displaced and plagued by significant theological questions about the faithfulness of God. Can God be trusted to keep the promises of the Covenant? This is the soil of dislocation, sorrow, mistreatment, and questioning.

e. Why (for what purpose) was the text written? The text announces the good news that God is coming to deliver the exiles. They are about to go home. So certain is the poet, that in verse 9 the poet speaks as if Jerusalem itself is the herald of the good news.

The poet asks the exiles to see themselves going home, no longer captives.

3. What would it feel like to be in that situation? Psalm 137 describes an aspect of the feeling of the exiles. I think I would feel like a plant pulled up by its roots and left on a hot asphalt parking lot on a July afternoon. Abandoned. Powerless.

4. Is it important for the congregation to experience something of the atmosphere and feeling of that situation in order to feel the full force of the text? I think it is. The situation of the main-line church in the United States is more like that of the Jews in Babylon who had adopted the Babylonian culture as their own than it is like the situation of those exiles who felt displaced. We are quite at home in our culture. Why should we want God to come when it feels like we have it made? The preacher may want to prepare the members of the congregation by helping them recall or imagine experiences of exile.

5. When I read this text, what do I:

a. See? The text contains a number of visual images. Verses 3–5 describe the coming of the Lord in imagery probably borrowed from the Babylonian new year festival in which a mammoth statue of the god Marduk was carried on a royal road through a wilderness area.[4] The image, familiar to the exiles, is transformed into a picture of God coming in glory, that is, in an act of deliverance. Verses 6–8 use the visual image of withering grass to describe the fate of the Babylonian captors. Verse 9 recalls the herald who would climb to a high place to announce the good news to the city dwellers so they could be ready to welcome God. Verses 10 and 11 place snapshots in counterpoint. Verse 10 pictures God as a victorious warrior with the spoils of the ravaged enemy, while verse 11 recollects the familiar association of God as shepherd—one who feeds, guides, heals, defends. The conquering warrior has the heart of the shepherd.

Why such a collage of images? All are organized under the rubric of verse 1—comfort. In the context of this carefully constructed poem, these images are intended to convey to the exiles the feeling of comfort. We might think of the poem as a kind of collage of comfort.

b. Hear? We hear the various voices crying. Muilenburg's widely followed hypothesis is that we may be privy to a discussion of the heavenly council.[5] In that council, God decides and decrees what will happen on earth. When the exiles hear the voices of the council, they take comfort in knowing that what is spoken is as if already accomplished. They can live on the basis of the announcement. In addition, we may hear the road crews at work in the wilderness, the wind blowing through the grass, the scout climbing the lookout.

c. Smell? I smell only those things characteristic of the places and events recalled in the poem, for example, the smell of sheep.

d. Touch? I touch only those things characteristic of the places and events recalled in the poem such as the crunch of withered grass underfoot.

e. Taste? I taste nothing.

6. *Is it important for the congregation to experience imaginatively any of these in order to feel the full force of the text?* Significantly, the poem speaks of comfort in vivid ways. The images themselves, in the context of what they would mean to the exiles, communicate the meaning of what it means to be comforted in exile. The preacher may want to draw pictures of "comfort" which are as vivid to contemporary exiles as these were to the captives. Can the sermon be set on a stage as comparably impressive to moderns as the heavenly council was to the exiles?

Suggestions for Further Reading

The histories of the biblical periods provide reliable accounts of "what was happening" in a given period in the life of a text. These include: John Bright, *A History of Israel,* 3rd ed. (Philadelphia: The Westminster Press, 1981); Siegfried Herrmann, *A History of Israel in Old Testament Times,* 2nd ed., trans. John Bowden (Philadelphia: Fortress Press, 1981); Bernhard W. Anderson, *Understanding the Old Testament,* 3rd ed. (Englewood Cliffs: Prentice-Hall Inc., 1975); Roland De Vaux, *The Early History of Israel,* (Philadelphia: The Westminster Press, 1978); Hans Conzelmann, *History of Primitive Christianity,* trans. John E. Steely (Nashville: Abingdon Press, 1973); Bo Reicke, *The New Testament Era,* trans. D. Green (London:

Black, 1968); Howard C. Kee, *The Origins of Christianity: Sources and Documents* (Englewood Cliffs: Prentice-Hall, 1973).

The introductions to the testaments will help with introductory questions, for example, Georg Fohrer, *Introduction to the Old Testament*, trans. David Green (Nashville: Abingdon Press, 1968); Otto Eissfeldt, *The Old Testament, an Introduction* (New York: Harper & Row Publishers, Inc., 1965); J. Alberto Soggin, *Introduction to the Old Testament*, rev. ed., trans. John Bowden (Philadelphia: The Westminster Press, 1982); Brevard S. Childs, *Introduction to the Old Testament As Scripture* (Philadelphia: Fortress Press, 1979); Werner G. Kuemmel, *Introduction to the New Testament*, rev. ed., trans. Howard C. Kee (Nashville: Abingdon Press, 1975); Robert A. Spivey and Moody D. Smith, *Anatomy of the New Testament*, 3rd ed. (New York: Macmillan Inc., 1982); Howard C. Kee, *et al.*, *Understanding the New Testament*, 3rd. ed. (Englewood Cliffs: Prentice-Hall Inc., 1973); and Norman Perrin and Dennis C. Duling, *The New Testament: An Introduction*, 2nd ed. (New York: Harcourt, Brace, Jovanovich, Inc., 1982).

A variety of incidental helps can illuminate the world of the text, among them: Martin Noth, *The Old Testament World* (Philadelphia: Fortress Press, 1966); Roland De Vaux, *Israel, Its Life and Institutions*, trans. J. McHugh (New York: McGraw-Hill, Inc., 1961); Denis A. Baly, *The Geography of the Bible*, new rev. ed. (New York: Harper & Row Publishers, Inc., 1974); *Oxford Bible Atlas*, 2nd. ed., edited by Herbert G. May and G. H. Hunt (New York: Oxford University Press, Inc., 1974); Yohanon Aharoni, *The Land of the Bible: A Historical Geography*, rev. and enlarged ed., trans. A. F. Rainey (Philadelphia: The Westminster Press, 1980); Yohanon Aharoni and Michael Avi-Yonah, *The Macmillan Bible Atlas*, rev. ed. (New York: Macmillan, Inc. 1977); Edward Lohse, *The New Testament Environment*, trans. John E. Steely (Nashville: Abingdon Press, 1976); Joachim Jeremias, *Jerusalem in the Time of Jesus: An Investigation into Economic and Social Conditions During the New Testament Period*, trans. F. H. and C. H. Cave (Philadelphia: Fortress Press, 1975).

4

Word Studies

The difference between the meaning of a word in its historical context and in its contemporary usage can be so great that it is as hard to determine the meaning as it is to read license plate numbers in Denver while standing on Pike's Peak fifty miles away. Like a telescope, a good word study can bring a distant and obscure word into sharp and clear focus.

A word study typically begins by tracing the origin of the word and then continues by outlining the successive phases of its use. With the help of a concordance, we follow the word through the Bible in circles of ever increasing size. First, we look up the word in passages which come from the same hand as the one under study. Then we look up similar passages from the same period of history, passages which are similar in form and content. We note the function of the word in quite different contexts and compare and contrast the word with others that are similar and opposite in meaning.

We try to position ourselves so that we hear a word with the same vitality and strength as it would have been heard by an ancient listener or reader. Because that is so often clarifying, and even surprising, word studies frequently walk the corridor directly from the study to the pulpit.

For example, for many moderns the word "prophet" means one who foretells the future. Thus prophecy is prediction of future events. A simple word study reveals that when chopped in half, the Greek word "prophet" is composed of two parts which mean "to speak" and "for." A prophet is one who speaks for someone else, notably God. A classical prophet speaks for God, interpreting the meaning of life and history from the divine perspective. On the basis of critical interpretation, the prophet may conjecture that certain future trends or events may take place, but the basic function of prophecy is interpretation.

In popular thought, love is an emotion, a warm flush of feeling. When I was five I loved my ice-cream cone. When I was sixteen, I loved anything in skirts. It was a surprise to learn that in some places in the Bible, love can mean the willful self-giving of one for another, quite apart from a cozy emotion.

We frequently find that words—especially theological words—which appear abstract and pale to us, were concrete and vibrant in their ancient uses. Edmund Steimle notices that many biblical words, especially abstractions, have had the "blood of action drained." [1]

Like a fine whetstone, word studies can bring a keen edge to the homiletical knife. The human mind usually thinks in the specific and concrete rather than in the abstract. When the preacher paints a concrete picture of the meaning of a word, that word will flash in the mind of the listener as if in technicolor. As the word takes on flesh and blood, it has a better chance of being absorbed by the listener.

We seldom hear the abstract noun "redemption" except in worship or in reference to what we do with trading stamps (at the redemption center we trade stamps for toasters). But in the last two centuries B.C.E., one of the Greek words for "redemption" *(apolutrosis)* meant to set free a captive for a price. A slave could be redeemed if the price of his or her worth could be paid. Criminals condemned to death and prisoners of war could be redeemed for a price. [2] This word, which appears in our language as an abstract noun has, in fact, a vivid action background. What would it mean to a slave to be redeemed? What does this suggest about the potential meaning of redemption to my congregation? Keep in mind that the discovery of such a background should not abort other careful analysis. How does the concept fit into the passage? How does it fit into the writer's thought as a whole? Often, then, the word itself begins to take on the full flesh of its meaning.

Further, many biblical words today belong almost exclusively to religious circles. To the uninitiated, words such as grace and righteousness may seem like an almost private, sacred speech. While the world of the Bible does not differentiate as sharply as we between the sacred and the secular, it is fair to say that many biblical words were arresting and powerful in their original settings precisely because they were used secularly. Baptized into the service of theology, they communicated the implications of the sacred in picturesque speech familiar from shop, home, marketplace, economics, and politics. Homiletically this suggests that preaching would recover increased biblical vitality if we would turn to secular ways of expressing theological truths.

Words change meaning from era to era, from culture to culture, and sometimes even from passage to passage. We need to make sure that the meaning we assign a particular word is appropriate to the text in which the word is found.

By way of example, in Psalm 119, "law" is used in a large and spacious sense to include all of God's revelation. In that Psalm law is whatever God has revealed for the instruction of all of God's creation. Law (Torah) can also be the story of God's gracious dealings with the Hebrews. While this larger sense is not altogether obscured, in Deuteronomy law usually has the more restricted sense of legislation which is to be obeyed. By the time of Christian literature, law could refer simply to the first five books of the Bible. Special care must be taken when interpreting Paul's use of the word "law" *(nomos)* because in one place he may emphasize the word's more specific aspect and in another place he may intend its larger sense. Like persons, passages are to be valued for their uniqueness.

Etymologies can be extremely provocative for preaching, but they should be used with caution. In the closet of history, the word "sin" *(hamartia)* has the famous meaning of failing to hit the mark.[3] In reference to athletic contests the word was used to indicate the act of throwing a spear at a target and missing. By analogy, to sin is to miss the mark. But that colorful etymology does not plumb the depth of Paul's use of the word to describe a power which causes the life of the creation to be broken and estranged from the Creator.

In Semitic speech names often have meanings that reveal something of the identity and purpose of the character. The name "Obadiah" means servant of the Lord. The name "Joshua" means YHWH saves[4] and in Palestinian Judaism of the first century C.E. "Joshua" was translated Jesus, which Matthew takes to be a way of interpreting the ministry of Jesus (Matthew 1:21).[5]

That caution should be taken in the use of etymologies is illustrated by the contradictory history of the name Jacob. At an early time, the name probably meant "may God protect."[6] But in the J tradition, the name Jacob takes another meaning that is explained by the birth of the twin brothers, Jacob and Esau. Jacob emerged from the womb, hanging onto the heel of his earlier-born brother, Esau, thereby trying to grab a share of Esau's birthright and blessing (Genesis 25:26). The writer intends for the name Jacob to be a play on the word "heel." Later, after Esau has been twice duped by Jacob, he comments that Jacob has been rightly named because ". . . he has supplanted me [i.e., been at my heel] these two times . . ." (Genesis 27:36). The storytellers have resurveyed the etymology for theological purposes. Later, of course, Jacob's name is changed to "Israel," which roughly means one who struggles with God.[7] From this perspective, a true Israelite is one who struggles with God.

Another aspect of word studies includes the identification of literary devices. The Song of Solomon repeatedly uses tender metaphors to describe the relationship of two lovers. When John the Baptist calls Jesus "the Lamb of God" (John 1:36), the phrase is hardly meant literally. Moses used blood when he sealed the Covenant at Mount Sinai (Exodus 24:6-8), but when Paul speaks of the blood of Jesus as making expiation for sin (Romans 3:25), the apostle uses a metaphor in which the word blood refers to death.

Thus, word studies can be extremely illuminating, but let us return to the analogy with which the chapter opened. To be able to read license plate numbers in Denver, while standing on Pike's Peak and using a telescope, will not tell us where the cars are going. For that we need a view of considerably wider angle, a view which other tools of exegesis can provide.

Key Questions

1. What are the fulcrum words on which this text turns?
2. How would the listeners or readers to whom this text was originally addressed have heard those words?
3. Is there so much distance between the congregation and the fulcrum words that the words will need to be explained in order to communicate with vitality and concreteness?
4. How can I concretely and vividly convey the meaning of the words to the congregation?

Case Study: Matthew 5:3

1. What are the fulcrum words on which this text turns? Blessed, poor in spirit, (reign) of heaven.

2. How would the listeners or readers to whom this text was originally addressed have heard those words?

a. Blessed. The lexicon and biblical dictionaries report that in classical Greek the word referred to monetary wealth as well as to inner happiness. Members of the upper social stratum were called blessed because they lived above the anxieties of those less wealthy. In canonical Jewish literature, to be blessed was to receive the favor and goodness of God, particularly in the way of material goods.[8]

Some attention is given to the literary form of beatitude in both canonical and intertestamental Jewish literature. The usual pattern is for the word "blessed" to be followed by a clause which describes those who are blessed. I note that a beatitude is a statement of fact (indicative) and not an exhortation (imperative).

Particularly in the context of beatitudes, in Christian literature, the word came to be related to the eschaton. The blessed are those who share in the joy of the reign of God. Indeed, they already experience something of its joy; a foretaste of the power of its coming is realized in their present existence. In contrast to "bless you," the casual expression when someone sneezes, the word "blessed" was charged with excitement, power, feeling.

b. Poor in spirit. Customarily, word studies begin by contrasting Luke's form of the beatitude "Blessed are you poor . . ." (Luke 6:20) with the form before us and commenting that Luke had in mind the economically impoverished, while the author of Matthew, by the addition of "in spirit," broadened the meaning to include all those who recognize their place before and their profound need of God. To be poor in spirit is to be aware of one's own poverty of spirit and deep reliance upon God.[9] I could stop the mechanics of word study at just this point. Certainly this interpretation would preach well: what could I do in the sermon to encourage the people to realize their profound dependence upon God and thus to enter the blessedness of the beatitude?

As I read through the word studies and commentaries, I see that both meanings (economic impoverishment and profound need of God) are possible. Several strata of canonical Jewish literature contain statements which describe God's concern for the impoverished as well as laws whose object is the care and well-being of the poor. But I also notice that in documents in the late canonical and intertestamental periods, the word "poor" can be used as a synonym for righteous.[10] This may reflect the actual economic and sociological condition. To oversimplify, Luke may have followed one Jewish tradition and Matthew another.

However, I notice that some of the secondary sources mention that the phrase "poor in spirit" may be used to denote voluntary poverty,[11] as perhaps at Qumran.[12] It is likely that those who entered the community on the edge of the Dead Sea surrendered their possessions to the common treasury of the community. Matthew may think that to be "poor in spirit" is to sell one's possessions and become voluntarily poor. But what purpose would there be in that?

I cannot make this judgment only on the basis of a word study. It must be checked against the larger pattern of Matthew's thought. First, the concordance leads me to three other occurrences of the word "poor" in the First Gospel, one of which supports my hunch (Matthew 19:16-26). Jesus tells the rich young ruler that if he would be perfect (*teleios,* an important Matthean description of the Christian life), he must sell his possessions, give the income to the poor and thus attain treasure in heaven. The young man is asked to use his possessions in the service of human need. (On the basis that "poor" is the name of the eschatological community, one could see the ruler giving his wealth to the service of the community, but this is hardly Matthean).

When the fishing folk are called to follow Jesus, they leave behind everything (4:18-22). The scribe is told to leave the dead to bury their dead (8:20-22).[13]

The life-style of Jesus and the Twelve (who function in this Gospel as a kind of paradigm for the church) is to live from day to day on the hospitality of the faithful who receive them (8:20; 10:9-11). The petition "Give us this day our daily bread" is existentially urgent.

Matthew highlights teaching which calls attention to the negative effect of wealth and possessions and asks the church members to relieve themselves of the self-serving anxieties that accompany ownership by relieving themselves of possessions (6:19-34, 19:23-30). Wealth itself seems to be an insulator from the gospel.[14] Further, the disciples are encouraged to understand the marvelous extent of the providential care of God for those who surrender their possessions for ministry (6:25-34; 7:7-12; 14:13-20; and 15:32-39 with 16:5-12).

c. Reign of heaven. This is another way of speaking of the reign (or kingdom) of God, the great transformation of the broken cosmos into the new order conformed in every respect to the will of God. The concept is so well known in theological circles as to require no explanation here.

3. Is there so much distance between the congregation and the fulcrum words that the words will need to be explained in order to communicate with vitality and concreteness? I would say that the concept of voluntary poverty for the sake of serving human need is almost entirely foreign to the typical main-line congregation in the United States. Therefore, it requires explanation.

4. How can I concretely and vividly convey the meaning of the words to the congregation? I need to keep in mind the form of the text: a beatitude, not an exhortation. I need to resist the temptation to exhort the people of the congregation to sell all that they have.

How could I do that with integrity as I stand in the pulpit in my pin-striped, all-wool suit, bankbooks bulging out of my back pocket? Instead, I can offer them indicative examples of those who, through voluntary poverty in the service of human need, have become blessed. I think of the Sojourners community in Washington, D.C., and the Koinonia farm in Georgia. Perhaps there are symbolic ways in which we can make such commitments. Above all, I need to remember to take my listeners seriously and not to run down their genuine struggles with the faith with the bulldozer of my newfound knowledge.

Suggestions for Further Reading

Limitations to the use of word studies are carefully outlined by James Barr, *The Semantics of Biblical Language* (Oxford: Oxford University Press, 1961). Among concordances the most useful general work covering both Jewish and Christian literature is still Robert Young, *Young's Analytical Concordance to the Bible*, rev. ed. (Grand Rapids: Wm. B. Eerdmans Publishing Co., 1982). A good concordance to apostolic literature is Clinton Morrison, *Analytical Concordance to the Revised Standard Version of the New Testament* (Philadelphia: The Westminster Press, 1979).

The major Bible dictionaries are *Theological Dictionary of the New Testament,* ed. Gerhard Kittel and Gerhard Friedrich (Grand Rapids: Wm. B. Eerdmans Publishing Co., 1964-76), 10 vols.; *Theological Dictionary of the Old Testament,* ed. G. Johannes Botterweck and Helmer Ringgren (Grand Rapids: Wm. B. Eerdmans Publishing Co., 1981); *The Interpreter's Dictionary of the Bible,* ed. George A. Buttrick (Nashville: Abingdon Press, 1964), 5 vols.; and *The Interpreter's Dictionary of the Bible, Supplementary Volume,* ed. Keith Crim *et al.* (Nashville: Abingdon Press, 1976). Excellent contemporary imagery, not always historically founded, is Frederick Buechner, *Wishful Thinking: A Theological ABC* (New York: Harper & Row Publishers, Inc., 1973).

5

Form Criticism:
The Individual Threads

Oral and written forms of expression tend to become stylized as they are associated with repeated life experiences. Although the contents vary, the form of business letters changes little from letter to letter. While the form may be the same, the content and feeling-tone of business letters may be quite different. A letter placing an order for 100,000 widgets may have a quite different tone from one that requests payment for a bill six months overdue. But the form does suggest the nature of the content. Seeing a business letter on my desk, I anticipate something very different from when I pick up a book of poetry written by someone imprisoned in Latin America.

The discipline of form criticism concludes that the form of individual units of biblical tradition is related to the function of those texts in ancient life in something of the same way that the form of a business letter is related to its function in modern life. Form criticism identifies particular genres of biblical literature (saga, wisdom saying, parable), as well as the characteristic elements and structures of the various genres, in order to determine how these units typically were used in the life of Israel and the early church.[1] These uses have implications for both the thrust and the form of the sermon.

Implications for the Thrust of the Sermon

The form critic is interested in both the ancient function of a text as well as in the characteristic structure and elements of its form. The function of a particular form (genre) in the ancient community may suggest an analogous function for that form for preaching in the contemporary church. (On the hermeneutic of analogy, see chapter 12.) Of course, the particular emphases and mood of a given text can be disclosed only by careful attention to the content, but knowledge of the function can suggest a general thrust for the sermon.

A review of the function of some representative forms from both Jewish and Christian literature will show how knowledge of the ancient function can suggest a contemporary function.

The saga is a story about a person, people, or place. Its purpose is to explain the identity of the people or why a certain place is the way it is. The saga locates people and places in time and space and invests them with meaning. The saga acts not only as a chronicle of the past but also as a mirror of the life of the people who relate the saga, so that when the tale is told, the hearers will respond, "That is my (our) story!" The saga thus acts to establish or form identity. For example, of the story of Jacob wrestling with the angel (Genesis 32:3-32), Gerhard Von Rad writes, "This event did not simply occur at a definite biographical point in Jacob's life, but as it is now related, it is clearly transparent as a type of that which Israel experienced from time to time with God. Israel has here presented its entire history with God almost prophetically as such a struggle until the breaking of the day."[2] A sermon based on such a saga would help the community find its own identity in the story. How do we, like Jacob, struggle with God; and how do such struggles lead to blessing, albeit blessing with a limp?

The prophetic warning functions to call erroneous behavior to the attention of those who practice it. The particular causes of chastisement are dated to the period in which the prophet spoke and include such things as self-serving life-styles, ethical failures in business and personal relationships, the neglect of the poor, alliance with pagan religion and similar violations of the Covenant. I know of no one who has a "bed of ivory" (Amos 6:4) or who "sells the righteous for silver" (2:6). In fact, a bed made of ivory sounds as if it would give me a backache and the closest I have come to real silver is hearing the market price on the news. The prophet, however, employs figures of speech which would have been familiar to his listeners to say that the opulent life-style of the upper classes is supported at the expense of the poor. Further disobedience will bring about "the ruin of Joseph." A sermon based on such a prophetic warning would call the similar behavior of our own culture to the attention of the middle and upper classes who practice it. It would be cast in images as graphic and stinging in our culture as those of Amos were in his.

A prayer of confession admits guilt and asks for forgiveness and deliverance. A sermon, of course, is not a prayer. But the preacher could use the text as an occasion to help the congregation awaken to its own guilt and to yearn for forgiveness. It is likely that circumstances which contribute to guilt will have changed. For example, I see no statues of Canaanite fertility deities on our streets. Yet I do know people who functionally worship realities other than God.

Many of the legal sayings of the Synoptic Gospels emerged from the primitive church's attempt to deal with practical problems. The setting in life of particular legal sayings is therefore quite specific, such as divorce (Mark 10:10-12) or relationships within the community (Matthew 18:15-17). The obvious implication of the function of a legal saying is to apply it to a specific aspect of modern church life. The obvious problem with this approach is that the specific problem with which a legal saying is concerned may not be a problem for the church today; and even if it is, the legal saying as it stands may not be the most appropriate way to address the problem. The question of the ritual washing of hands, for instance, is hardly a live issue in contemporary churches in the United States (Mark 7:1-8). For the text to have meaning for the contemporary church, the preacher needs to identify issues in our church and culture which function in our communities in the way that the issues of the text functioned in the first-century church.

The function of the historical stories (and legends) is not just to recall (or to create the impression of) historical events but also to make the listeners aware of the meaning of the events so that the listeners will want to appropriate the significance of the stories for themselves. The narratives are carefully constructed, both theologically and artistically, to communicate the significance to first-century hearers. For example, a purpose of the account of the baptism of Jesus (Mark 1:9-11) is more than recollecting the day when Jesus was immersed by John in the River Jordan. Using the motifs of the heavens ripping apart, the divine voice and the elusive symbol of the dove, the narrator says, "The new age is beginning. In baptism you become a part of this age!" In preaching from such accounts, our purpose is not to evaluate their historicity but to translate their meaning into terms our congregations will want to appropriate.

A doxology expresses a sense of blessing, praise, and thanksgiving to God as in Revelation 5:12. A sermon that is faithful to the function of the doxology will do the same.

The function of a catalogue of virtues (Galatians 5:22-23) is to outline the character of a particular way of life. The list is meant not to be exhaustive but to be representative. Preaching on such a list will neither settle into a series of word studies nor will it become an exhortation to the congregation to work toward developing those traits in themselves. It will characterize the life outlined in the list as vividly in modern terms as the list of virtues did in ancient terms.

Implications for the Shape of the Sermon

In addition to helping identify the thrust of the sermon by calling attention to the form of a text, form criticism may help in the shaping of the sermon. A particular form (structure) is not arbitrary or accidental but intentional and closely tied to life experience. The structure is a means whereby the text carries out its intended function.

Further, since the beginning of the twentieth century, studies in the relationship between human experience and expression have increasingly stressed the continuity between *what* is said and the *way* it is said.[3] In the language of form criticism, we might say there is a close relationship between function (what is said) and form (the way it is expressed). To change the form of a text is to change its function.

The form of the text can therefore suggest a form for the sermon. In some cases this may be quite specific, while in other cases the suggestion will be more general.

Form critics speak of the "typical features" of a form. These are elements that are usually present in texts classified as a certain form. A typical feature of the beatitude, for instance, is the presence of the word "blessed." Every text so classified, however, may not have every typical feature. An individual text may drop one feature and add another.

The typical features may furnish a structure for the sermon. The form of the healing miracle typical of the Synoptic Gospels is a clear example. These stories have a typical fivefold structure (although the last two elements are not always included):

1. The description of the setting of the story and the condition of the patient.
2. The confrontation with the healer.
3. The healing itself (a spoken word, a touch, and the like).
4. Evidence that the healing has taken place (the patient sees, walks, rises from the dead, and the like).
5. The response to the healing (a gasp of amazement, praise, jubilation).

The sermon itself might not be an extended narrative, but it could unravel in the same way as the miracle story. What is our "illness?" How do we confront the source of healing? What is the evidence that healing has taken place?

Narrative forms, such as saga, myth, legend, historical narrative, scholastic dialogue, parable, do not unload their meaning all at once like a dump truck depositing a load of rich dirt in the backyard. Instead, they invite the listener to join them as they impart their meaning bit by bit.

Non-narrative forms can also prompt a structure for the sermon, although the continuity between what is said and the way it is said may be less obvious than in the case of narrative. In some cases this will lead to a one-to-one correspondence between the elements of the form and the outline of the sermon. In other instances, especially in the case of short forms (like the wisdom sayings, many of which are comprised of only one sentence), the form may suggest a tone and general movement which the preacher could create in the sermon.

The individual song of thanksgiving, found frequently in the Psalms, furnishes an example of a non-narrative form in which the structure of the form can structure the sermon in a one-to-one fashion. Using Psalm 116 as an example we can see such a structure.

1. Introduction (vv. 1-2). The speaker announces the intention of the psalm, namely to give thanks because God has performed a great deed in the life of the speaker.

2. Review of the crisis and rescue (vv. 3-11). The recounting typically involves three elements, not necessarily in this order.
   a. Picture of the crisis.
   b. The cry of the speaker for help.
   c. God's act of deliverance.
   In this case, the author has suffered intensely and felt the cold breath of death.

3. Conclusion (vv. 12-19). The speaker reiterates gratitude to God. The author says that he or she will offer a "sacrifice of thanksgiving" at the temple.

A sermon could easily follow such a structure. The content, of course, would develop from the life of the community in which the sermon is preached, and it should be conveyed as graphically as the psalm.

The proverb is more difficult. A proverb may be as short as a single sentence. In such short form, the sentence is typically composed of two parts called members (or limbs). These may be in one of three types of relationships: synonymous parallelism, antithetical parallelism, or progressive (synthetic) parallelism. In the first, the second member restates the meaning of the first member in different words. The restatement slows down the mind and causes it to savor the meaning. Antithetical parallelism juxtaposes two opposite ideas: the first member states an idea and the second member its opposite. Progressive parallelism builds one idea upon another in the manner in which a high rise building is constructed—rising floor upon floor.

The structure of a proverb may suggest the structure for the sermon. Progressive parallelism, for example, may outline the sequence in which the major ideas of the sermon unfold. On the other hand, such forms may suggest a tone and general movement. Antithetical parallelism makes its point by means of the experience of contrast, and occasionally that experience is quite shocking. The sermon, similarly, could provide the congregation with an experience of contrast.

The rhetorical features of individual proverbs (as indeed, of individual texts) are worth close attention. The proverb is grounded in life experience, and preaching from proverbial texts should stay close to life experience. If the proverb is indicative, then let the sermon be indicative. If the proverb makes use of analogy, then let the preacher observe the life of his or her community for an equally arresting analogy. If the proverb leaves the mind in shock, well.
. . .

Key Questions

1. What form is this text?
2. What was the function of that form in the ancient community?
3. Does the function of the text suggest a thrust for the sermon?
4. Does the form of the text suggest a form for the sermon?

Case Study: Mark 2:23-28

1. What form is this text? Rudolf Bultmann calls it a controversy story. Martin Dibelius calls it a paradigm. As usual, Bultmann's designation is the more widely used.

2. What was the function of this form in the ancient community? The controversy story sets forth, in dramatic form, a conflict. In this text the conflict exists between the church and the surrounding culture, especially between the church and Judaism. The function of this controversy story is to vindicate the life and ministry of the church in the face of controversy. The means of vindication is to present the charge through the mouth of an opponent and to present an answer (in the form of a saying) from the mouth of Jesus.

This particular story witnesses either to a conflict between the church and the synagogue over sabbath practice or to an intra-church controversy between Jewish Christians who still observe the sabbath and other Christians who did not. The function of the story is to justify and establish the church's freedom for ministry on the sabbath.

The narrative appears to have developed in more than one stage. Essentially the first stage appears in verses 23 and 24, also in verse 27. Later stages include the incorporation of verses 25 and 26 and the Christological saying of verse 28. The pericope probably circulated in much of its present form before Mark received it.

The specific violation of sabbath custom is the plucking of grain by the disciples on the sabbath. Early readers or listeners could have assumed that the reason for plucking the grain was the hunger of the disciples.

While canonical Jewish literature contains no direct prohibition of picking grain on the sabbath, some Jews of the first century equated "plucking" with harvesting. Since harvesting was work and work was forbidden on the day of rest, plucking grain was unacceptable.

Jesus is pictured as responding to the critique of the Pharisees by calling to mind the famous incident in which David and his friends, starving, broke into the temple and ate the bread of the Presence. David, a great example of Jewish piety, violated the law for the sake of human need.

Verse 27 indicates the "true" purpose of both sabbath and law. According to verse 28, the effect of the presence of the Son of man is to realize the true meaning of both. Post-resurrection hearers of such a story would realize that his presence is still alive and at work. In the living presence of Jesus, response to human need takes precedence over custom.

3. Does the function of the text suggest a thrust for the sermon? As far as we know, the church and synagogue today are not in conflict over plucking grain on the sabbath. But the values of the church are (or should be) in conflict with the values of the surrounding culture. The controversy story suggests a sermon which focuses on a conflict between the values of the church and the values of the culture.

In particular the story pictures a church in trouble with its culture because it responded to human need in a way which violated the culture's standards and expectations. Are there such instances in the life of your own community?

4. Does the form of the text suggest a form for the sermon? The typical features of the controversy story do indeed offer a possible structure for the sermon. Illustrated by Mark 2:23-28, they are:

1. The introductory narrative which sets the stage on which the story takes place. This narrative is brief and specific, describing a situation or stating an idea which challenges the dominant culture (2:23).
2. The opponent's question is expressed clearly but economically. The question is not cavalier. It raises an issue which is significant to the ethos represented by the questioner (2:24).
3. The saying of Jesus is the climax toward which the story points. It explains why the church's ministry is justified (2:25-29).

In using such a structure, the preacher will want to be as specific in his or her situation as the controversy story was in its own. A simple adaptation might be made like this.

1. Recall an aspect of the life or ministry of the church which cuts across the grain of the dominant values of our culture. So to speak, how do we pluck grain on the sabbath?
2. Articulate the conflicts between the culture and the church. How does our culture ask, "Look, why do they do that which is not lawful?"
3. Relate the saying of Jesus to the situation described in the conflict. How does he give us a new understanding of our situation?

Suggestions for Further Reading

General summaries of canonical Jewish forms are found in Otto Eissfeldt, *The Old Testament: An Introduction,* (New York: Harper & Row, Publishers, Inc., 1965); Georg Fohrer, *Introduction to the Old Testament,* trans. David Green (Nashville: Abingdon Press, 1968). Still basic on the narrative forms of the Pentateuch is Hermann

Gunkel, *The Legends of Genesis,* (New York: Schocken Books, Inc., 1964). On the genres within the Psalms see B. W. Anderson, *Out of the Depths: The Psalms Speak for Us Today* (Philadelphia: The Westminster Press, 1974).

The various types of prophetic speech are catalogued in Claus Westermann, *Basic Forms of Prophetic Speech,* trans. Hugh White (Philadelphia: The Westminster Press, 1967). While not focusing particularly on form criticism, one of the best introductions to the wisdom literature is James L. Crenshaw, *Old Testament Wisdom: An Introduction* (Atlanta: John Knox Press, 1981).

The most comprehensive catalogue of forms in the Synoptic Gospels is still Rudolf Bultmann, *The History of the Synoptic Tradition,* 2nd ed., trans. John Marsh (Oxford: Basil Blackwell, 1972). If possible, one should compare Bultmann's examination of a specific passage with that of Martin Dibelius, *From Tradition to Gospel,* trans. Bertram L. Wolff (New York: Charles Scribner's Sons, 1971). On the Fourth Gospel, a good resource is Raymond E. Brown, ed., *The Gospel According to John* (New York: Doubleday & Co., Inc., 1966, 1970), 2 vols. The special characteristics of Acts are set aside in connection with specific passages in Ernst Haenchen, *The Acts of the Apostles, a Commentary,* trans. R. Wilson (Philadelphia: The Westminster Press, 1971). A useful guide to the types of material employed by the letter writers is Archibald M. Hunter, *Paul and His Predecessors* (Philadelphia: The Westminster Press, 1961). A concise statement of the status of research in the epistles is William G. Doty, *Letters in Primitive Christianity,* ed. Dan O. Via, Jr. (Philadelphia: Fortress Press, 1973). G. B. Caird, *The Revelation of St. John the Divine* (New York: Harper & Row Publishers, Inc., 1966) clarifies the forms in the last book of the Bible.

A general introduction is Klaus Koch, *The Growth of the Biblical Tradition,* (New York: Charles Scribner's Sons, 1968). Other general overviews are Gene M. Tucker, *Form Criticism of the Old Testament* (Philadelphia: Fortress Press, 1971) and Edgar V. McKnight, *What Is Form Criticism?* (Philadelphia: Fortress Press, 1969), as well as Gerhard Lohfink, *The Bible, Now I Get It: A Form Criticism Hand-*

book (New York: Doubleday & Co., Inc., 1979) and (from a literary perspective) Leonard L. Thompson, *Introducing Biblical Literature: A More Fantastic Country* (New York: Prentice-Hall, Inc., 1978). One can also see the articles in *The Interpreter's Dictionary of the Bible, Supplementary Volume,* ed. Keith R. Crim (Nashville: Abingdon Press, 1976).

6

Redaction Criticism: The Whole Picture

A painting is meant to be viewed as a whole. In a particular work we may notice that a figure's hands have such a special character and intensity that our eyes are drawn repeatedly to the hands. As we step back and look at the whole canvas, we find that it is carefully composed to focus our attention on the hands. Shading, color, lines are all used to direct our gaze.

In much the same way, biblical writers designed their materials to call attention to certain themes, perceptions, and theological realities. Redaction criticism seeks to view a biblical document as a whole, paying attention to the special emphases of its author who is sometimes called a redactor or editor.[1]

Preaching the Piece in Light of the Whole

Whereas the form critics tended to view the redactors of biblical books as collectors who did little more than paste together independent pieces of tradition (like miracle stories and sayings) to form the larger work, we now regard the redactors as authentic authors and genuinely creative theologians. The editors recast the traditions in their own style and gave the traditions interpretations peculiar to their own situations in order to speak specifically to the situation of the community to whom the document was addressed.

Because biblical preaching customarily arises from a single pericope, a major contribution of redaction criticism is to let us see the meaning of the individual text in light of its meaning to the whole work.[2] When preaching from the viewpoint of redaction criticism, the preacher will interpret the piece from the perspective of its use in the whole.

A critical question is "For what purpose does the author use this pericope?" The author's interpretation may be quite different from that of the historical event in which the text arose or from that of the oral tradition.

For example, both Luke (15:1-7) and Matthew (18:12-14) tell the famous parable of the lost sheep. The parable probably came from the lips of the historical Jesus, perhaps in response to criticism from his opponents regarding his ministry to the religiously and culturally unacceptable. By giving the parable a strategic literary context and by shaping it in light of the situation of their churches, each Gospel writer gives the parable a different interpretation. Luke uses it as a vehicle to encourage joy over repentance. Matthew puts the parable in the context of a discourse on the nature and responsibility of the Christian community and uses the parable as a picture of the way in which community leaders are to seek after a member who strays.

While we commonly associate redaction criticism with the Gospels and Acts, the principle of interpreting a piece in light of the whole may be applied to any writing in which older pieces of tradition are taken up by an author. For instance, in the case of the first five books of the Bible, we can see how the traditions of the Yahwist and the Elohist were taken up and edited according to the need of the priestly writer to address the situation of the exiles in Babylon. From the redactional point of view, we put ourselves in the situation of the exiles and ask, "What would it mean to hear the awesome description of creation in Genesis with its affirmation of the absolute sovereignty of God, a sovereignty which extends far beyond that of the gods of Babylon?"

Multiple Possibilities for Preaching in Each Text

Although not always apparent to a casual reader, a text in its canonical form is often the result of a history of development—

rather like a house to which numerous changes and additions have been made. In conjunction with other critical disciplines, redaction criticism helps us see the historical stages in the development of a text.

In the case of some texts we can see three (or more) levels of development, each of which has its own integrity and nuances of meaning which should be honored in exegesis and preaching. Consider the following:

1. *The level of a historical event.* In the case of the historical Jesus, this would be what he actually said or did. In the case of a historical narrative, it might be what actually took place at Gilgal.

2. *The level of the life of the oral tradition.* This is the use of the passage in the preaching and teaching of the church, or in the life of Israel, before it was redacted. Some texts have quite complicated histories of development.

3. *The redactional level.*

While a pastor may not be able to engage weekly in such a full-scale analysis, a good commentary or monograph will call attention to the history of the development of the text. In addition, the introduction of a good commentary will outline the redactional themes and concerns of the work.

We can, thereby, see multiple possibilities for preaching in many texts; for each level of the development of a text can inform a separate sermon. Indeed, to mush together the nuances of meaning from different levels may be to violate the integrity of each.

On a given Sunday morning, a text from the Synoptic Gospels might inspire five different sermons. One could come from the life of the historical Jesus, another from the oral tradition, and one each from those whom we call Matthew, Mark, and Luke.

This process of development can be seen clearly as we unravel the development of Mark 2:18-22. According to criteria established for determining an authentic saying of Jesus, we can see that the pericope contains such a saying, around which the church has created a setting, all of which has been taken up by the Gospel writer.

1. From the level of the historical Jesus comes the saying in verse

19*a*. "Can the wedding guests fast while the bridegroom is with them?"[3] Jesus makes use of a common first-century symbol of salvation—the wedding feast—to say that in his presence, common religious practices, such as fasting, no longer apply. Instead, in the larger context of the ministry of Jesus, the people are invited to join in the joy of the dawning rule of God. A possibility for preaching is obvious. Who would fast while a party is going on?

2. The reference to the Pharisees appears to be a Markan addition. Beyond that we can detect two levels of the use of the story in the oral tradition. Verses 18 and 19*a* describe one situation while verses 19*b* and 20 describe another.[4]

The church apparently did not practice fasting in its early years and soon found itself in conflict with John the Baptist's disciples who fasted fervently. Fasting was an important means of prayer and preparation for the coming rule of God. Therefore, at the first stage of the oral tradition, the church used verses 18 and 19*a* as a means of justifying its not fasting. A sermon from this level of the tradition might ask, "How does the contemporary church come into conflict with our culture over a question like that of fasting?"

Verses 19*b* and 20 indicate that the church reintroduced fasting as a part of its life. This section explains why that reintroduction was appropriate. The bridegroom is no longer present.

3. At the redactional level, Mark seems to have several themes in mind as he uses the pericope. By adding the Pharisees, it becomes part of Mark's growing polemic against the Jewish religious establishment, probably thereby witnessing to the deteriorating relationship between Mark's church and official Judaism about the time of the fall of Jerusalem. More significantly, Mark adds verses 21 and 22 to the conflict story. This has the effect of completely relativizing the practice of fasting (and by implication, all such institutions of Judaism). For Mark the future of the church is the Gentile mission. To preach from the viewpoint of Mark may be to pose the question to the contemporary church. Do we continue old and honored customs which are no longer appropriate to our mission? Do we need new skins for new wine?

Consider, as well, the story of the victory at the Red Sea as the children of Israel were making their way from bondage to freedom. While that event is given a prose account in Exodus 13:17–14:30, we focus on the poetic narrative of Exodus 15:1-21.

1. At the historical level we can no longer determine exactly *what* happened at the Red Sea. Apparently, a small band of Hebrew slaves who were escaping from Egypt were on the verge of capture, perhaps even annihilation, on the shore of the Red Sea. Something made it possible for them to escape.[5]

2. The event at the Red Sea was given an important theological interpretation in one of the oldest fragments of poetry in canonical Jewish literature, the Song of Miriam, Exodus 15:21.[6] This song, an example of a hymn of triumph, attributes the escape at the Red Sea to the marvelous work of God, and it was used in cultic life (perhaps as early as Moses) to celebrate the victory. Apparently such songs were used in cultic assemblies in order to inspire warriors preparing for holy war. As God defeated Pharaoh at the Red Sea, so the warriors can take confidence that God will bring victory through them.[7] A sermon on the text at this level might seek to inspire the congregation with the confidence that through them, victories (though not necessarily of a warlike character) may still be won in situations that look as bleak as that of the Red Sea.

3. The Song of Miriam was gradually expanded into the hymn of Exodus 15:1-18 and was used in the liturgy of the cult.[8] In its present form, it presumes the conquest of Canaan and perhaps even the erection of the temple. Verses 17 and 18 indicate that the purpose of the poem is not simply to recall a historical occurrence but ''an event in past history has been extended into present time and freed for every successive generation to encounter.''[9] Preaching from this level may want to help the congregation claim the rescue at the Red Sea as part of its own story: ''We, too, were there. Not only were we there, but we also encounter that same reality today.''

Key Questions

An important redaction critical question is ''For what purpose does the author use this pericope?'' Because the answer to this question is not always obvious from the text itself, or even from a commentary, I suggest questions which are designed to facilitate one's own redactional study. Such an analysis is most effective when done in concert with a historical analysis described in chapter 3.

Redaction criticism is made easier when we can identify the approximate composition of the tradition before it reached the hand of the editor.[10] Then we can clearly see how the writer reshaped the tradition. (This is not always possible either because the editor has composed the piece entirely or because it may be so completely reworked as to be unrecoverable. Thus, in the questions that follow, the first two are less important than the remainder.)

1. Can we identify the approximate shape of the text before it reached the author's hand?[11]
2. How has the author reshaped the tradition?
3. Does the literary context cast light on the interpretation of the text by the redactor?[12]
   a. What comes before?
   b. What comes after?
   c. What is the effect of the placement of the text?
4. What are the central or significant motifs/words/persons in the pericope?
5. How are these significant elements used and what meaning do they have in the rest of the literature produced by the redactor?
6. In light of the reshaping, the context, and the meaning of the major motifs, how is the redactor addressing the community through the text?
7. What situation in the redactor's community might have called forth this address?
8. Does the community to which the sermon will be preached find itself in a similar situation?
9. Does the redactor's message appropriately address the community to which the sermon will be preached?

Case Study: Luke 14:15-24

1. Can we identify the approximate shape of the tradition before it reached Luke's hand? The original text appears to have been a parable which began with verse 16b. The conclusion of the parable seems originally to have been simpler, perhaps containing only one invitation to unexpected guests and reading similarly to Matthew's conclusion (Matthew 22:1-10).[13] Prior to reaching Luke, the story was probably a simple parable of reversal.

2. How has the author reshaped the tradition? Luke has given the parable its present context by attaching a saying (Luke 14:15) to the parable and reworking the conclusion so that the poor and dispossessed become the unexpected guests. These are important elements in Luke's use of the story.

3. Does the literary context cast light on the interpretation of the text by the redactor? I think the placement of the text is very important to its interpretation.

a. What comes before? The parable is told in the context of a dinner (Luke 14:1) which becomes an occasion of controversy between Jesus and the Pharisees (14:2-5). In 14:7-11 Jesus criticizes the behavior of his fellow guests who sought seats of honor at the dinner, thus exalting themselves. In the pericope which immediately precedes the parable, Jesus gives an injunction to pay special attention to the poor, maimed, lame, and blind (14:12-14). The parable is told in direct response to the beatitude spoken by a pious Jew. The beatitude is a way of speaking of participation in the age of salvation. Thus, the parable seems, in part, to be a comment on who will participate in the age of salvation.

b. What comes after? Luke 14:25-27 contains hard sayings on the nature of discipleship. The sayings are followed by the parables of counting the cost of becoming a disciple of Jesus (vv. 28-33). These seem to have the purpose of correcting faulty notions of what it means to partake in the reign of God as it is being manifested in the ministry of Jesus. In Luke 15 we find a series of parables which justify the concern of Jesus for sinners and outcasts and suggest God's special interest in them. Luke 16 graphically portrays the obstacle created by the possession of wealth to entering the reign of God.

c. What is the effect of the placement of the text? The parable becomes an illustration of the exhortation of Luke 14:12-14 and a corrective to the conventional attitude typified by the beatitude of Luke 14:15. Jesus' listeners (or Luke's church) should be concerned about outcasts because God is concerned about them.

4. What are the central or significant motifs/words/persons in the pericope? They are the feast and the invitation to the poor, maimed, lame, and blind.

5. How are these significant elements used and what meaning do they have in the rest of the literature produced by the redactor? The feast seems to function in the traditional way as a metaphor for the age of salvation.[14] Throughout the Gospel of Luke, as well as the book of Acts, we find Luke directing our attention to God's concern for the poor. Indeed, the church itself is depicted as a fellowship characterized by aggressive ministry in behalf of the poor. In the reign of God, social and economic barriers to fullness of life disappear (see Luke 1:52-53; 4:16-30; 6:20; 7:22; 7:36-50; 18:22; 19:8; Acts 6:1ff.).

6. In light of the reshaping, the context, and the meaning of the major motifs, how is the redactor addressing the community through the text? Luke is encouraging his church to adopt an aggressive ministry to the poor. The life of the church is an instrument through which the poor, maimed, lame, and blind can enter the reign of God. Luke seems to advocate not only full and open relationships between the rich and the poor but also the redistribution of wealth. In this way both the circumstances of poverty and the obstacle to obedience, created by the possession of wealth, are reversed.

7. What situation in the redactor's community might have called forth this address? Without direct evidence, such reconstruction is always tenuous. It would seem, however, that Luke's church is a mixed community in which the wealthy hoard their wealth for their own self-serving interests while the poor are left destitute. In any case, as the rule of God dawns, that situation changes.

8. Does the community to which the sermon will be preached find itself in a similar situation? I would say that in North America, most main-line congregations are more segregated economically than Luke's church. In any case, many white main-line protestant congregations seem to demonstrate little of the significant sharing of resources with the poor for which Luke calls. If the issues of the parable are projected onto a national or international scale, we can quickly see similarity of situation.

9. Does the redactor's message appropriately address the community to which the sermon will be preached? I believe that the membership of white, main-line Protestant North American congregations manifest much the same attitude toward wealth and exclusivism as Luke's church. Therefore, Luke's use of the parable seems appropriate.

Suggestions for Further Reading

The basic introduction to redaction criticism is Norman Perrin, *What is Redaction Criticism?* (Philadelphia: Fortress Press, 1969). A summary of continental scholarship to the mid-1960s is Joachim Rohde, *Rediscovering the Teaching of the Evangelists* (Philadelphia: The Westminister Press, 1969). An early redaction critical analysis by a North American is H. C. Kee, *Jesus in History* (New York: Harcourt, Brace, Jovanovich, Inc., 1970).

The basic redactional study of Matthew is Günther Bornkamm, *et.al., Tradition and Interpretation in Matthew* (Philadelphia: The Westminster Press, 1963). A provocative and more contemporary analysis is Jack D. Kingsbury, *Matthew: Structure, Christology, Kingdom* (Philadelphia: Fortress Press, 1975) and his proclamation commentary, *Proclamation Commentaries: The New Testament Witness for Preaching Sermons,* ed. Gerhard Krodel (Philadelphia: Fortress Press, 1977).

A pivotal examination of Mark is Willi Marxsen, *Mark the Evangelist,* trans. Roy A. Harrisville (Nashville: Abingdon Press, 1977). Another seminal work is Howard C. Kee, *Community of the New Age* (Philadelphia: The Westminster Press, 1977). Along the same lines as Kee but with profound attention to hermeneutical matters is Neill Q. Hamilton, *The Recovery of the Protestant Adventure* (New York: The Seabury Press, Inc., 1981). A good commentary from the redactional perspective is Eduard Schweizer, *The Good News According to Mark,* trans. D. Madvig (Atlanta: John Knox Press, 1970).

The beginning point of modern Lukan studies is Hans Conzelmann, *The Theology of St. Luke* (Philadelphia: Fortress Press, 1982). Updates on Luke include I. Howard Marshall's two important works, *Luke: Historian and Theologian* (Grand Rapids: The Zondervan

Corp., 1971) and *Gospel of Luke* (Grand Rapids: Wm. B. Eerdmans Publishing Co., 1978). The best traveling companion to Acts is Ernst Haenchen, *The Acts of the Apostles, a Commentary* (Philadelphia: The Westminster Press, 1971).

Easily the most comprehensive guides to the Fourth Gospel are the two volumes by Raymond E. Brown, *The Gospel According to John* (New York: Doubleday Publishing Co., 1966, 1970). Brown's colleague, J. Louis Martyn, furnishes other incisive studies, *History and Theology in the Fourth Gospel,* rev. ed. (Nashville: Abingdon Press, 1979) and *The Gospel of John in Christian History* (Ramsey, N.J.: Paulist Press, 1978).

While "redaction criticism" as a term has not been applied widely to the work of scholars interpreting canonical Jewish literature or the epistolary corpus of Christian literature, insights very similar to those of redaction criticism emerge in the better commentaries and in the work of literary critics.

7

Structuralism: The Text Manifests Deep Structure

A series of five floor plans is used in the construction of a housing development of several hundred homes. While homes built according to one floor plan are interspersed with homes built according to the other four floor plans, only the five floor plans are used. The houses do not look exactly alike because they are built with different materials and are trimmed in different colors. Over the years, the trees and shrubs mature, additions are built onto the homes, and the homes reflect the character of their owners. While the houses change, the basic floor plans remain limited to the original five, and, to the careful eye, are discernable.

In a similar way, structural critics contend that human consciousness expresses itself in only a few basic patterns or structures.[1] These patterns underlie verbal forms of expression rather like the floor plans underlie the construction of homes in the housing development. While the content of texts varies significantly, a text will ordinarily manifest one of the basic patterns which are repeated from culture to culture.[2] A grasp of that structure may inform both content and structure of the sermon.

However, two problems prevent us from soaring immediately aloft in an updraft of structural interpretation. First is the diversity of approaches to structural exegesis. Instead of a common vocabulary and a uniform method of textual analysis, we find an array of approaches as scattered as the pellets of a fired shotgun shell. The second problem is comprehensibility. Structural exegesis is frequently presented in language and diagrams which are reminiscent of the secret vocabulary attributed to the Gnostics of antiquity. To the uninitiated it is a mystery. Like the hang glider pilot, the preacher needs a good sense of the terrain before leaping into the wind.

The Text Embodies Deep Structure

The goal of traditional exegesis is to understand the meaning of the text in the light of its historical context. In contrast, the structuralist seeks to understand the text as a text, without reference to what the author "intended." Structural analysis focuses on the elements which are already contained within the text, for the text contains within itself the data for understanding its underlying structure. If I had the assignment of making a diagram of the plumbing in Mr. Jones's house, I would need to look at the house itself.

In the vocabulary of structuralism, the traditional method of study is called *diachronic* exegesis while structuralism is called *synchronic* exegesis. In diachronic investigation, one takes account of all that has come before, so that one sees the text as the evolution of a series of historical events. Its meaning is determined by its place in those events. In synchronic exegesis, the meaning of the text is determined by the interdependence and interrelationship of the elements of the text which are already in the text itself. We do not rummage in the attic trunk of history to gather materials with which to clothe the text with meaning; instead, we observe the interaction of the components of the text.

Every text is composed of discrete units, often called "lexies." A lexie is a single unit of thought or action which makes sense by itself, without reference to other discrete elements.[3] Structural criticism centers on the analysis of the interaction of the lexies which comprise the text.

In the Bible, a lexie may be a part of a verse, a whole verse, several verses, a chapter or even a book, depending upon the text under consideration. From the parable of the father and the two sons, we note some examples:

Lexie 1: There was a man who had two sons.

Lexie 2: And the younger of them said to his father, "Father, give me the share of the property that belongs to me."

Lexie 3: And he divided his living between them.

Each lexie achieves meaning only in relationship to the other lexies in the story.

Structuralists speak of studying the interaction of the elements of the text in two different perspectives: *syntagmatic* and *paradigmatic*. A syntagmatic reading of the text is one which follows the text from beginning to end in linear fashion, noting the interrelationship of the various components. In the case of the parable of the father and the two sons, a syntagmatic reading notes that as the parable opens, the father and the two sons are in close relationship. The relationship is broken when the younger son takes his share of the inheritance and goes to the far country. A moment of recognition leads to the reunion of father and younger son.

The paradigmatic perspective concentrates not on the linear sequence of events and thoughts, but on the larger themes, thoughts, and associations that may be evoked by individual elements of a text. A word or phrase may evoke a larger cultural structure whose understanding is necessary for the interpretation of the text. In the parable of the woman who lost one of her ten coins, the lost coin is given meaning because it is part of a larger structure—the monetary system. The mention of the lost coin cannot be adequately understood apart from its place in the larger structure.

Two Models of Structural Analysis

While structural critics work from several different models of textual analysis, two models are of special importance: (1) the model of mythic analysis developed from the linguistic studies of Ferdinand de Saussure and from the structural anthropology of Claude Lévi-Strauss; and (2) The "actantial" model which originated in the work of A. J. Greimas. Both should be regarded as illustrations of two ways (among many) by which one can conduct a structural analysis.

1. The basic structure of reality, according to Lévi-Strauss, is

that of binary opposition. The fundamental binary opposition is that of life against death. Nearly all other contradictions mirror this fundamental one, for example clean in opposition to unclean, heaven in opposition to earth, cooked (culture) in opposition to raw (savage). In their raw form, these contradictions threaten life and order with chaos and ultimately with death.

The purpose of mythic texts is to mediate between these contradictions so that the threat of chaos is overcome and we can understand life as a whole. The myth relates the oppositions to one another in such a way that the contradictions no longer represent a threat to life and order; the relationship of binary opposition is transformed. Thus, the first step in structural analysis of a mythic text is to identify the binary opposition which underlies the text. The second step is to make an account of the way in which that opposition is overcome.

The critical question is "How does the myth transform the contradiction?" In order to answer this question, we break the myth into basic units similar to the lexie, but called "mythemes."[4] Then we note how the mythemes and bundles of mythemes are related to each other.

Lévi-Strauss expresses this transformation in the form of an equation.[5]

$$F_x(a):F_y(b)::F_x(b):F_{a-1}(y)$$

In this complex equation, the symbolic elements represent realities.

> F = a general symbol for function.
> a and b = states of being or action.
> x and y = particular functions.

$F_x(a)$ represents the function of a particular state of being or action; while $F_y(b)$, $F_x(b)$, and $F_{a-1}(y)$ represent the functions of other beings or actions. The function x is related to the subject (a) in one side of the binary opposition while on the other side the function, y is related to the subject (b). In the mythic text this opposition is transformed so that the function x is linked to subject (b) and this new relationship is in secondary (but not absolute) opposition to subject y which now has the function of (a).

Perhaps an illustration will clarify this seeming doublespeak.

Behind the notion of the Covenant in the Deuteronomic theology is the binary opposition between death and life. Obedience to the Covenant brings life whereas disobedience brings death. The binary opposition is mediated in the fact that the Covenant is sealed by the death of an animal whose blood is spread at an appropriate place.

$$F_{obedience}(life):F_{disobedience}(death):F_{obedience}(death):F_{life}(disobedience)$$

Ironically, in the making of a covenant, one can say that an act of death (killing the animal) brings life. Much the same type of mythic structure informs Christian reflection on the death of Jesus. The helpless are saved precisely by that most helpless act.

2. The structural analysis of narrative texts is facilitated by an actantial model designed by A. J. Greimas. The model relates six actants (persons or spheres of action) which are found within almost every narrative.

Sender——— Object——— Receiver

Helper——— Subject ———Opponent[6]

The actants are simply defined.

Sender   = one who wishes to communicate a message or an action.
Object   = whatever the sender wishes to communicate.
Receiver = the person for whom the communication is intended.
Helper   = that which helps the sender.
Subject   = the agent through whom the communication is facilitated and who may be called upon to deal with the negative input of the opponent.
Opponent = the force which opposes the communication.

As the arrows indicate, the transaction moves along three axes. The first is the axis of communication which consists of the sender wishing to communicate the object to the receiver. The second is the axis of power in which the helper provides the power necessary for the subject to facilitate the communication. This facilitation is complicated by the opponent. The third axis is that of volition, that is, the plot by means of which the subject helps the transaction of communication take place.

Take the case of the healing of blind Bartimaeus (Mark 10:46-52). Jesus (the sender) wants to give sight (the object) to Bartimaeus (the receiver). Faith is the helper which allows Jesus to achieve communication which is hindered by the crowd (the opponent).

Jesus———— sight———— Bartimaeus

Faith———— Bartimaeus ——Crowd

Preaching the Deep Structure

Of course, one cannot preach in the language of Lévi-Strauss or Greimas. Imagine the response of a middle-class, provincial congregation to a topic like "Overcoming the Binary Opposition Between the Cooked and the Raw."

In preaching the objective is neither to name the underlying structures nor to describe them. Rather, in preaching we want to let the underlying structure of the text shape the sermon appropriately in content and structure. Thus, the sermon will lead the mind of preacher and congregation in the same pattern as that of the text, thereby touching the contemporary audience at the feeling level. The sermon may manifest a one-to-one correspondence between the structure of the text and the outline of the sermon, or it may lead to a correspondence of theme. I suggest three ways by which structural exegesis may inform preaching.

First, in the view of Lévi-Strauss, in the case of texts which have a mythic character, we can often specify the binary opposition which underlies the text and the manner in which the text overcomes the opposition. These would become the theme for the sermon. In the example of the clean and the unclean, we would first want the congregation to experience that tension and subsequently to find resolution.

Second, in the case of a narrative, we might apply the actantial model of Greimas. The sermon would move along the relationships of the various axes so that the structural relationships and transformations of the narrative are recreated in the sermon. Because the actants within the text do not always follow one another in linear fashion, one may or may not follow the outline of the text. We could use the three axial movements as an outline for the sermon.

Third, because the models of structural exegesis are pluralistic, one need not be bound to an established model. At the risk of oversimplifying, we might say that structuralism helps us to see how and why a text moves from one place to another. Our grasp of the text is enlarged as we understand this movement. As a way of conducting independent structural analysis, the following might be illuminating:

1. Note the situation at the beginning of the text.
2. Note the situation at the end of the text.
3. Note the transformations that take place as the text moves from beginning to end.

While such a working model might not name binary opposition or actantial structure, it could easily touch the deep structure of the text.[7]

Key Questions

Because of the diversity of approaches to structural criticism, it is difficult to formulate comprehensive key questions. The following questions are an attempt to incorporate basic insights of the discipline:

1. What are the basic units of the text?
2. What is the situation at the beginning of the text?
3. What is the situation at the end of the text?
4. What is the basic opposition underlying the text?
5. Do elements of the text evoke larger structures which have a role in the text?
6. What transformations take place as the text moves from beginning to end?
7. How does the underlying opposition and its resolution suggest structure and content for the sermon?[8]

Case Study: 1 Kings 17:7-16[9]

1. What are the basic units of the text?
   a. And after awhile, the brook dried up, because there was no rain in the land (v.7).

b. (8-9a). Then the word of the LORD came to him, "Arise, go to Zarephath, which belongs to Sidon, and dwell there" (vv.8-9a).

c. "Behold, I have commanded a widow there to feed you" (v.9b).

d. So he arose and went to Zarephath (10a).

e. And when he came to the gate of the city, behold, a widow was there gathering sticks (v.10b).

f. And he called to her and said, "Bring me a little water in a vessel, that I may drink" (v. 10c).

g. And as she was going to bring it, he called to her and said, "Bring me a morsel of bread in your hand" (v.11).

h. And she said, "As the LORD your God lives, I have nothing baked, only a handful of meal in a jar, and a little oil in a cruse" (v.12a).

i. "And now, I am gathering a couple of sticks, that I may go in and prepare it for myself and my son, that we may eat it, and die" (v.12b).

j. And Elijah said to her, "Fear not; go and do as you have said" (v.13a-b).

k. "But first make me a little cake of it and bring it to me, and afterward make for yourself and your son" (v.13c).

l. "For thus says the LORD the God of Israel, 'The jar of meal shall not be spent, and the cruse of oil shall not fail, until the day that the LORD sends rain upon the earth'" (v.14).

m. And she went and did as Elijah said (v.15a).

n. And she, and he, and her household ate for many days. The jar of meal was not spent, neither did the cruse of oil fail, according to the word of the LORD which he spoke by Elijah. (v.15b-c).

2. What is the situation at the beginning of the text? Israel and the Gentile lands are in drought and famine. The lives of Elijah and the widow are threatened.

3. What is the situation at the end of the text? Both Elijah and the widow have plenty of food and water.

4. What is the basic opposition underlying the text? The basic opposition is between famine and plenty and ultimately between death and life.

5. Do elements of the text evoke larger structures which have a role in the text? In addition to the basic structure of famine/plenty, the text evokes the structures of the relationship between Israelite (clean) and Gentile (unclean) as well as that of man (Elijah) and woman (the widow).

6. What transformations take place as the text moves from beginning to end? The Israelite man is sent to Gentile territory for food. The Gentile woman follows the seemingly futile instructions of the Israelite male to prepare food when she has no supplies. The Gentile woman then becomes the source of food and water for the Israelite male. The agent of these transformations is the word of the Lord.

7. How does the underlying opposition and its resolution suggest structure and content for the sermon? In order for the text to touch the deep structures of the consciousness of the congregation, the sermon might deal with the basic opposition of famine/plenty. The congregation needs to feel the tension of that opposition and then needs to feel how that opposition is overcome. The particular content of this narrative relates the overcoming of the secondary oppositions (Israelite/Gentile, man/woman) to the resolution of the major opposition. In the face of profound need, God transforms the basic structures so that life prevails.

Suggestions for Further Reading

Two volumes, read in sequence, provide a substantial working introduction to structuralism: Daniel Patte, *What Is Structural Exegesis?*, ed. Dan O. Via, Jr. (Philadelphia: Fortress Press, 1976) and Daniel Patte and Aline Patte, *Structural Exegesis—From Theory to Practice: Exegesis of Mark 15 and 16 Hermeneutical Implications* (Philadelphia: Fortress Press, 1978). A collection of articles of unusual clarity on this subject is found in *Interpretation* 28 (1974). The journal *Semeia* contains many articles from the structural perspective; see especially volume 1 (1974).

The basic works of Saussure, Lévi-Strauss, and Greimas should be read by those who wish to work in detail in structural study, for example, Ferdinand de Saussure, *Course in General Linguistics,* trans. Wade Baskin (New York: McGraw-Hill Book Co., 1966); Claude Lévi-Strauss, *The Elementary Structures of Kinship,* ed. Rodney Needham, (Boston: Beacon Press, 1969); *The Raw and the Cooked* (New York: Octagon Books, 1970); *The Savage Mind,* (Chicago: University of Chicago Press, 1966); *Structural Anthropology,* trans. Monique Layton, (New York: Basic Books, Inc., Publishers, 1976); A. J. Greimas *et al., Sign. Language. Culture.* (The Hague: Mouton, 1970); "Elements of a Narrative Grammar," *Diacritics* (March, 1977), pp. 23-40. On Greimas, see Jean Calloud, *Structural Analysis of Narrative,* ed. William A. Beardslee, trans. Daniel Patte (Philadelphia: Fortress Press, 1976); and V. Propp, *Morphology of the Folktale,* ed. Louis A. Wagner, trans. Laurence Scott (Austin: University of Texas Press, 1968). More general introductions are Robert Scholes, *Structuralism in Literature: An Introduction* (New Haven: Yale University Press, 1974) and Roland Barthes, *Writing Degree Zero* and *Elements of Semiology* (New York: Hill & Wang, 1977).

Editor Alfred M. Johnson, Jr., is making extraordinary efforts to make structural literature available to English readers, including a 2,000-item bibliography available from the Clifford Barbour Library, 616 N. Highland Ave., Pittsburgh, PA 15206. Among the excellent collections he has edited (and translated) are: *Structural Analysis and Biblical Exegesis* (Pittsburgh: The Pickwick Press, 1974); *The New Testament and Structuralism: A Collection of Essays* (Pittsburgh: The Pickwick Press, 1976); *Structuralism and Biblical Hermeneutics* (Pittsburgh: The Pickwick Press, 1979).

Other important studies include: Edgar V. McKnight, *Meaning in Texts: The Historical Shaping of a Narrative Hermeneutics* (Philadelphia: Fortress Press, 1978); Robert M. Polzin, *Biblical Structuralism: Method and Subjectivity in the Study of Ancient Texts* (Philadelphia: Fortress Press, 1977); Robert C. Culley, *Studies in the Structure of Hebrew Narrative* (Philadelphia: Fortress Press, 1976); David Jobling, *The Sense of Biblical Narrative: Three Structural Analyses in the Old Testament* (Sheffield, England: University of

Sheffield, Department of Biblical Studies, 1978); Robert Detweiler, *Story, Sign and Self: Phenomenology and Structuralism as Literary-Critical Methods,* William A. Beardslee, editor (Philadelphia: Fortress Press, 1978); Dan O. Via, Jr., *Kerygma and Comedy in the New Testament: A Structuralist Approach to Hermeneutic* (Philadelphia: Fortress Press, 1975).

One should be aware of critiques of structuralism, for example, Paul Ricoeur, *The Conflict of Interpretations: Essays on Hermeneutics,* (Evanston: Northwestern University Press, 1974); Erhard T. Guttgemans, *Candid Questions Concerning Gospel Form Criticism: A Methodological Sketch of Fundamental Problematics of Form and Redaction Criticism,* trans. William G. Doty, (Pittsburgh: The Pickwick Press 1979).

8

Sociological Exegesis:
Text and Social Reality

The adaptation of sociological methods to exegesis is one of the most recent disciplines to put on its cleats and take to the track of biblical interpretation.[1] The sociologically oriented biblical critic insists that a text can be fully understood only when we grasp the social world(s) in which the text was given birth and in which it moved.

Through the use of established sociological methods, adapted from studies like those of Max Weber, Emil Durkheim, Ernst Troeltsch, Bryan Wilson, Peter Berger and Thomas Luckmann, sociological exegesis attempts to discose the social dynamics at work in the formation of biblical texts.[2] These dynamics can be instructive for preaching.

From Sociology to Sermon

At the risk of oversimplification, I propose a commonsense approach to the use of sociological insights in sermon preparation which is based on the notion that many important clues for social analysis are found in the biblical text itself or can be found in the background materials readily available in the basic reference works on biblical study. I call attention to six aspects of sociological analysis which are significant for homiletical preparation: (1) the description of social facts; (2) the social history against which a text is read; (3) the social position of the community to which the text was addressed; (4) the social situation within the community to which the text was addressed; (5) the "social strategy" of the text; (6) the relationship between the social situation of the community to which the text was written and the language and symbolism of the text.[3]

1. Social facts include concrete artifacts (housing, food, climate) which affect social life as well as basic life activities like vocation. Because of the unfamiliarity of the modern churchgoer with the world of the Bible, it may be helpful to describe pertinent social facts in the course of the sermon.

For example, a description of the life and work of a tentmaker would give the listener a concrete picture of what Paul means when he says that he worked night and day in Thessalonica. This labor as a tentmaker, in order not to burden the community, is in sharp contrast to that of the religious leaders, apparently begging itinerants whose poverty was regarded as a sign of religious legitimacy, whose visit to the congregation prompted the Thessalonian letter.[4]

2. By relating such facts to the political, economic, cultural, and religious events of the time, one can write a social history. For instance, for many years it was widely assumed that the early church was largely lower class; but research of the last decade indicates that, at least in urban areas, the churches by the time of Paul may have been much more heterogenous and may have included large numbers of the middle class and even some of the upper class.[5]

While sociologists of the Bible, to this point, have been more interested in general trends than in the exegesis of individual pericopes, social history can be of value in the interpretation of single texts. Ezra's concern for the dissolution of marriages to foreign women (Ezra 9-10) can be fully appreciated only against the social history of family life in Israel and the particular role assigned to the family to strengthen the community against compromise with non-Israelite culture. Awareness of the social history of the place and role of women in the society of the ancient Near East, especially the denial of religious instruction to women in some of those societies, gives the story of Jesus' visit with Mary and Martha a dimension far beyond that of the contrast between the busy Martha and the quiet Mary (Luke 10:38-42).[6]

As in the case of the description of social facts, it may be helpful to describe salient aspects of the social history of a text in the sermon. In the story of Mary and Martha, a description of the place of women in ancient culture would help listeners grasp the revolutionary nature of the rabbi Jesus giving instruction to women.

3. The social position of the community to which the text was written is usually one of two types. The community may be in a position of such power and authority that the values and practices of the community reflect and support the values of the larger culture; or the community to which the text was directed was frequently in a minority position within the culture and was often antithetical to the larger society.

During the years of the Conquest, for instance, Israel's social position was that of a struggling minority; but during the Monarchy, Israel was in the position of dominance. During the time of Hosea, the community for which the text was spoken had assimilated values and practices which were antithetical to the tradition of Israel, whereas during the Exile the community was estranged from the values of the larger Babylonian culture. The community for which Matthew was written appears to have been a sect, with profoundly Jewish roots, that was apart from the mainstream of either the Jewish or Gentile culture.

Awareness of the social position of the community to which the text was written can help us compare the position of that community with the position of the community in which the sermon will be preached. While they embrace persons of various economic and social strata, most main-line congregations in the United States reflect and support the values and practices of the larger cultural scene.

Groups in affluent social situations tend to be receptive to materials which confirm and conserve their place in society. They tend to resist calls for substantive change in values and life-style. Majority groups tend to interpret their traditions in a way that makes life as comfortable for them as possible. A saying like "Sell all that you have and give to the poor" is spiritualized and emptied of sociological power. In contrast, minority groups will often challenge the values and life-style of the dominant culture, even to the point of calling for the overthrow of the prevailing society.

Thus, realizing that I am in a position of affluence, I can be aware of my tendency to use a text to support my own social position. When I come upon texts written for groups in other social positions, I can take account of our differing social perspectives. The nature of this account will become clearer as I pay attention to the social strategy of the text.

4. The social situation within the community to which the text was written can generally be said to fall into one of two categories: unified stability or a condition in which the community is in conflict with itself. Being aware of such conflict can help us grasp some of the nuances within texts.

Behind the Book of Amos stands, in part, conflict between the well-to-do upper classes of Israelite society and the impoverished peasantry that was actively exploited by the wealthy. Amos attempts to overcome the conflict and the predictable destruction of the social fabric by calling attention to covenantal responsibility. The Covenant places individuals and groups in trans-class responsibility to each other.

The Corinthian congregation is a classic example of a community which has become fragmented. While the fragmentation is partly over theological differences, Gerd Theissen has shown that it also reflects class conflicts between upper and lower economic groups. This is especially clear in 1 Corinthians 11:17-34 in which the eating customs of the wealthy and those of the lower classes have come into direct conflict. Paul attempts to moderate the conflict by offering an eschatological understanding of social reality in which the customs of class are replaced by the vision of the eschatological community.[7]

A practical correlative to historical analysis is the analysis of the social situation within the community to which the sermon will be preached. Is that situation similar or dissimilar? Can the text suggest an appropriate social effect for the sermon within the life of the contemporary church? Such questions pertain to the social strategy of the text.

5. A text will often have a "social strategy," that is, an intended social effect on its recipients.[8] A text may elicit a specific social response.

One social strategy is to confirm the present situation. As the postexilic community was reconstructing Judaism and the priestly party was claiming power, the writer of Chronicles wished to support that claim. Hence, the writer interprets David, ark, and temple so as to confirm the priestly party as rightful heir of the sacred tradition.

Another social strategy is to ask the community to adjust to the present situation, even when that situation is hostile. Luke, for instance, uses the book of Acts to help the community to make peace with the Gentile culture. He also seeks to encourage the Gentile culture to welcome the church as a nonthreatening part of the social milieu.

A third social strategy is to call for the reform of the present situation. Elijah, seeing unacceptable devotion to Baal within the Israelite community, a devotion epitomized by Jezebel, sought to reform the community. Indeed, one can characterize reform as a prophetic social strategy.

Another social strategy is to call for the replacement of the present social order by a new social reality. The Gospel of Mark, like other apocalyptic literature, seems so alienated from the present social order that reform is hardly possible. Instead, the community's social hope is centered in the apocalyptic coming of the rule of God.

Of course these strategies are not always "pure." James Wilde has shown that while Mark looks for the replacement of the old order by the new, the Gospel also asks the community to accept its present alien status in the old age. On the basis of Mark 13, one can infer that suffering at the hands of local authorities is intrinsic to that alien status. Mark helps his community understand and accept its suffering by holding up as its model the suffering of the Son of man. Although the Son of man suffered, the community expects him to return in glory, a glory that the community hopes to share. In the meantime the community is to engage in ministry in behalf of others, particularly through exorcism and other acts of healing.[9]

The preacher's concern would be with how the social strategy of the text suggests an appropriate social strategy for the sermon. Nowadays, to use a text to address a contemporary community in a social situation other than that of the community to which the text was written can lead to distortion and misrepresentation. A text intended to strengthen a community alienated from its culture can have exactly the opposite of its intended effect when used to comfort a group that is in a position of power and affluence.

For example, Zechariah 9-14 was apparently written to a minority group that was being pushed out of the reorganization of official Jewish life after the Exile. To this group, apparently poor and politically powerless, the prophet quoted the Lord.

I will strengthen the house of Judah,[10]
and I will save the house of Joseph.
I will bring them back because I have compassion
on them,
and they shall be as though I had not rejected
them;
for I am the LORD their God, and I will answer
them.
Then Ephraim shall become like a mighty warrior,
and their hearts shall be glad as with wine.
—Zechariah 10:6-7a

To preach the text as a source of social strength and confirmation to those whose place closely resembles the social position of those to whom the text was originally opposed is to reverse its meaning.

This raises an important question. How can a text intended for one social group speak today to a group in a remarkably different position? A church in a position of social affluence, the position of most white main-line North American congregations, may need to hear a text of challenge or reform as a challenge to its own life. On top of Mount Carmel might we not be standing among the priests of Baal? Further, such a church may need to hear a text written to support a marginal group as a text which challenges the life of the strong community. Consider Daniel 3. While by faith and tradition we are fourth cousin to Shadrach, Meshach and Abednego (representatives of the struggle against Hellenism), by social position we are first cousin to Nebuchadnezzar. The same church may need to read texts of confirmation and support as a reminder that God is the source of abundance and prosperity and that such blessing is the twin of Covenant responsibility.

When making a judgment about an appropriate social strategy for the sermon, one may need to remember that a part of the social strategy of the text is to increase the faithfulness of the community to which the text was written. While the specific content of what it means to be faithful in a given situation can be discovered only by vigorous theological reflection, we can generally say that for Jewish communities of the canonical period, faithfulness meant living up to Covenant responsibility while Christian communities intended to live in the light of the new age. The most elementary Bible dictionary will reveal that both are social realities.

Since increased faithfulness is also the goal of the sermon, one can assess the relationship of the social strategies of text and sermon only within the larger theological framework of faithfulness. The crucial hermeneutical component is the analysis of the social situation to and in which the sermon will be preached. What social strategy will increase the faithfulness of the community? Of course, a single sermon will hardly be able to transform a given social structure. However, sermons can contribute significantly to an overall strategy in ministry.

6. The relationship between the social situation of the community and the language and symbolism of the text is expressed in a simple principle: A community creates language (and systems of symbols) to interpret and account for its experience of social reality. Therefore, from the vantage point of our later time, from the language and symbolism of the text, we can ascertain the community's experience of social reality.

Apocalyptic communities provide exceptionally clear examples. It is now established that apocalyptic literature develops its first and strongest roots in communities which are alienated from the prevailing society. Apocalyptic literature reflects the experience of alienation at the same time that it attempts to invest that experience with meaning. In the early Palestinian Christian communities, for instance, we find the saying "The first shall be last and the last shall be first." This statement is obviously generated by a community whose experience is that of being "last." The language of the text places that experience in a framework of meaning which will allow the community to survive its situation of "lastness."

While apocalyptic literature provides examples of unusual clarity, the same phenomena can be seen elsewhere. Recent research has pointed out that the Johannine community was separated from the mainstream of both Jewish and Gentile cultures. Wayne Meeks finds that the Johannine Christ is withdrawn from, and even against, "the world." This Christ thus represents the position of the community in the larger culture and reinforces the community's perception of its place in society.[11]

The experience of social collapse is the seedbed of the symbolic universe of First Isaiah. To use the symbolism of chapter five, the community which had been a fruitful vineyard has produced wild grapes. In Isaiah's view, the social collapse meant also the collapse of the symbolic universe in which the nation had understood itself as elect and blessed, that is, a fruitful vineyard. Into the symbolic vacuum, Isaiah introduces the idea of the faithful remnant, a small community of the faithful within the degenerate larger society. The image of the faithful remnant thereby reflects and justifies the social position of the mini-community.

In addition to reflecting social reality, the language and symbolism can also affect a community's perception of, and initiatives within, social reality. By offering the community a new perception, the community may be able to change its social reality.

In Ezekiel 40-48 the prophet offers a vision of the new temple. A social purpose of the vision is to offer the community a world of symbolism as an alternate to that of its broken state. When the community begins to live on the basis of the symbolism of the changed situation, that situation can become a social reality.

In the Gospel of Matthew, the central message of Jesus is the dawning of the royal rule of God. In the imagery of that rule, the

Gospel writer offers the church a fresh vision of reality characterized by such things as forgiveness and healing.

The language and symbolism of the contemporary church is largely constructed on the basis of its own social reality in dialogue with the tradition. Through the canon the church has inherited the language and symbolism of communities whose social realities were far different. A part of the contribution of this perspective to preaching is to help the preacher bring the symbolic worlds of ancient and contemporary communities into appropriate conversation.

The contemporary church is hardly in the position of being a "faithful remnant," but the language of Isaiah may cause us to ask, "What is happening to the symbolic universe of our church and culture?" Does the notion of being a faithful remnant offer the church an alternate symbolic universe within which to understand itself?

The white main-line church is hardly last in the social order, but that symbolic world may ask us to consider those who are. Does the language of lastness, with its accompanying social experience, challenge our own language and social experience? If we began to live out of the image of the royal rule of God as the basis for social reality, what would happen to the fabric of the human community?

Key Questions

1. Does the text or background about the text suggest that a description of some social facts may be pertinent to the interpretation of the text?
2. Does the text or background reading suggest that an aspect of social history might be important to the interpretation of the text?
3. What was the social position of the community to which the text was addressed?
4. What was the social situation within the community to which the text was written?
5. What was the social strategy of the text? For example:
   a. Does it confirm the present situation?
   b. Does it ask the community to adjust to the present situation?
   c. Does it call for a reform of the present situation?

    d. Does it describe the replacement of the old order with a new?
6. What was the relationship between the social reality of the community to which the text was written and the language and symbolism of the text?
7. Is the congregation to which the sermon will be preached in a social position that is similar or dissimilar to that of the community to which the text was addressed?
8. Does the strategy of the text in its ancient setting suggest an appropriate social strategy toward which the sermon might aim?
9. Do the language and symbolism of the text suggest a function for the language and symbolism of the sermon?

Case Study: 1 Peter 2:11-12[12]

1. Does the text or background about the text suggest that a description of some social fact(s) may be pertinent to the interpretation of the text? We need to know the meaning of "alien." In the past we assumed that it had a metaphorical meaning in which earthly existence (as aliens) was in contrast to the heavenly hope. A fresh look at the ancient context suggests that it may refer to those who are outside the mainstream of the social order—or social aliens. One could almost speak of aliens as a social class.

2. Does the text or background reading suggest that an aspect of social history might be important to the interpretation of the text? As I review the life-style of aliens in the ancient world, I discover that their social history was one of displacement. Apparently they had no permanent homes, and they wandered from place to place.

3. What was the social position of the community to which the text was addressed? Their social position was that of being on the fringe of society, bereft of political, legal, social, or even conventional religious standing. The author of First Peter seems to assume that the church to which the letter is addressed is such a community.

4. What was the social situation within the community to which the text was written? A reading of the whole letter implies that while the community does not seem to be internally fragmented, it does seem to be suffering, perhaps at the hands of outsiders.

5. *What was the social strategy of the text?* The social strategy of the text is for the community to look forward to the replacement of the old order with a new social reality. In the meantime, the community is to maintain itself as the "household of God" (see 1 Peter 4:17). The function of this household is to serve as an alternate social structure to the community's place in the larger culture .

6. *What was the relationship between the social reality of the community to which the text was written and the language and symbolism of the text?* The language of the letter as a whole allows us not only to reconstruct the social situation but also to see that the author interprets the social situation in such a way as to give meaning to the community's state of alienation and suffering.

7. *Is the congregation to which the sermon will be preached in a social position that is similar or dissimilar to that of the community to which the text was addressed?* Most main-line congregations are in social positions remarkably dissimilar to that of the Petrine community. In fact, one could say that today's church is in the position of the Hellenistic culture in which the ancient church was trying to survive.

8. *Does the strategy of the text in its ancient setting suggest an appropriate social strategy toward which the sermon might aim?* While the contemporary church cannot classify itself as alien in the technical sense of First Peter, it may want to constitute itself as a social alternative to the prevailing culture. Certainly, North American middle- and upper-class culture supports values and practices which are inimical to those of the Christian community. The church cannot withdraw from the larger society, but it could model "the household of God" for the larger culture.

9. *Do the language and symbolism of the text suggest a function for the language and symbolism of the sermon?* Perhaps the sermon could offer the church an alternate perception of reality in which the church could see itself as a household of God in the Petrine sense. The function of the symbol in the sermon would be to give the church a new vision of social reality out of which it might live.

Suggestions for Further Reading

The bibliography of biblical studies utilizing sociological methodology is burgeoning. Many of the volumes cited here also contain excellent bibliographies. A helpful introduction is the series of articles in *Interpretation* 37, no. 3 (1982).

In addition to standard Bible dictionaries and encyclopedias, basic sources for social facts include Roland De Vaux, *Ancient Israel,* vol. 1, *Social Institutions,* vol. 2, *Religious Institutions* (New York: McGraw-Hill Book Co., 1965); Joachim Jeremias, *Jerusalem in the Time of Jesus,* trans. F. H. and C. H. Cave (Philadelphia: Fortress Press, 1975); Martin Hengel, *Judaism and Hellenism: Studies in Their Encounter in Palestine During the Early Hellenistic Period,* trans. John Bowden (Philadelphia: Fortress Press, 1981).

Among social histories, important basic contributions include Norman K. Gottwald, *The Tribes of Yahweh: A Sociology of the Religion of Liberated Israel* (Maryknoll: Orbis Books, 1979); Robert R. Wilson, *Prophecy and Society in Ancient Israel* (Philadelphia: Fortress Press, 1980); Paul D. Hanson, *The Dawn of Apocalyptic: The Historical and Sociological Roots of Jewish Apocalyptic Eschatology,* rev. ed. (Philadelphia: Fortress Press, 1979); Robert M. Grant, *Early Christianity and Society* (New York: Harper & Row Publishers, Inc., 1977); Abraham J. Malherbe, *Social Aspects of Early Christianity* (Baton Rouge: Louisiana State University Press, 1977).

A leader in the field is Gerd Theissen whose works are fundamental, especially *Sociology of Early Palestinian Christianity,* trans. John Bowden (Philadelphia: Fortress Press, 1978) and *The Social Setting of Pauline Christianity: Essays on Corinth,* trans. John H. Schutz (Philadelphia: Fortress Press, 1982). An influential essay is John G. Gager, *Kingdom and Community: The Social World of Early Christianity* (New York: Prentice-Hall, Inc., 1975). Howard C. Kee provides basic introduction with his *Christian Origins in Sociological Perspective: Methods and Resources* (Philadelphia: The Westminster Press, 1980). From the double viewpoint of both methodology and content, significant studies are Wayne Meeks, *The First Urban Christians* (New Haven: Yale, 1983) and John Elliot, *A Home for the Homeless: A Sociological Exegesis of 1 Peter, Its Solution and Strategy* (Philadelphia: Fortress Press, 1981).

A basic work dealing with the relationship of social reality to language and symbolism is Peter L. Berger and Thomas Luckmann, *The Social Construction of Reality: A Treatise in the Sociology of Knowledge* (New York: Doubleday Publishing Co., 1966).

9

Liberation Theology: Exegesis from Below

As a responsible member of our household, I regularly take my turn going to the supermarket. Because my favorite foods are fried (potatoes, eggs, fish, okra) and sweet (chocolate-chip cookies, deep-dish desserts), I almost unconsciously load them into my cart. Frequently, however, I do not even notice foods (like spinach) that are really nourishing.

In much the same way, the things of which we are conscious and unconscious, the things we like and dislike, influence what we find—and do not find—in the Scriptures. Sometimes we need to have themes and ideas called to our attention. Liberation theology can help us to focus on previously unnoticed dimensions of the biblical text and to identify the presuppositions with which we read the Bible.

A Change in Perspective

Liberation theology is not a specific exegetical discipline like form criticism. It is a particular theological point of view which originated among people who are economically, socially, and politically oppressed. Liberation thought emerged from the attempt to understand God's word and activity in relation to the disfranchised and destitute.

This attempt involves a fundamental change of perspective from which to interpret the Bible and its relationship to the structures of society.[1]

When we in places of privilege and power read the Bible, we like to find confirmation of our view of the world and support for our values and life-style. As a white, middle-class, "first-world" male, I would unconsciously find in the Bible a divine blessing on my place in society. Thus, I can find in the Bible justification for sexual, racial, and national superiority. I can even explicitly use the Bible to explain the condition of the poor and to retard serious effort on their behalf. After all, "For you always have the poor with you . . ." (Mark 14:7), and the Bible does say, ". . . be content with what you have . . ." (Hebrews 13:5). We tend to find in the Bible a mirror image of our own values which are largely private and individualistic,[2] and we tend to overlook aspects of the biblical corpus which challenge the presuppositions of our individual and corporate lives.

Liberation theologians point out that when we read the Bible from the position of those on the underside of life, namely the poor and oppressed, other aspects of the biblical experience come to light. Consider the words "The earth is the LORD's and the fulness thereof . . ." (Psalm 24:1). From the vantage point of a middle-class Christian who owns a cabin beside a spring-fed river in the Ozark Mountains, the text may describe his or her feeling about nature. "Something this great could have come only from God!" But to an impoverished peasant whose cheap labor bankrolls the opulence of the plantation owner, the text may be revolutionary. "The land is not the property of the landlord! The land belongs to the Lord and should benefit all the Lord's children."

Among the most important liberation themes are: (1) the assertion that God's fundamental activity is the liberation of persons from situations of oppression; (2) the bias of God toward the poor (and against the rich); (3) the fact that oppression is often the result of the function of a political and economic system; and therefore, liberation means not only a change in the lives of individuals but also a change in the way a society may be organized (i.e., systemic change).[3] The goal is justice.

The Text as Liberating Word

In order to determine whether a particular biblical text can speak a liberating word, the preacher needs to become conscious of the oppressive and liberating realities associated with a text. Many texts presuppose for their understanding social situations of oppression, powerlessness, injustice. The word of liberation to the oppressed may at first seem to be a word of judgment on the oppressor, but when fully perceived the act of oppressing someone else is itself oppressing to the oppressor. Therefore, liberation of the oppressed means liberation of the oppressor as well.

This perspective raises a practical problem for preaching. Most sermons in main-line pulpits arise from a single biblical pericope. Liberation theologians, on the other hand, frequently work more with themes than with individual texts. Perhaps examples will illustrate how the liberation perspective can make us sensitive to the oppressive and liberating realities in individual texts.

In the story of the Exodus, Pharaoh (and the ruling class) support their lavish building projects and luxurious life-style on the basis of the slave labor of the Hebrews. The existence of the Hebrews is characterized by affliction, bondage, enforced birth control. The oppression of slavery clamps a chokehold on all of reality—personal, political, economic. Thus, when God determines to break Pharaoh's hold on the Hebrews, that determination is a political act involving not only the correction of their immediate situation (freedom) but also the creation of a new social structure (the land flowing with milk and honey).

The story of the Exodus is a paradigm for the activity of God in history. Elements of humankind are repeatedly oppressed in ways similar to the oppression of the Hebrews, but from the story of the Exodus, we learn that God's fundamental work is liberation. The hermeneutical task is the identification of concrete situations of oppression and, conversely, of concrete instances of liberation.

The famous vision of the restoration of the valley of dry bones (Ezekiel 37) was given to the community in exile, a community that was politically powerless. In Ezekiel 37:11 the feeling of the people is voiced: ". . .'Our bones are dried up, and our hope is lost; we are clean cut off.'" This is the language of estrangement. Against the background of an oppressed community, chapter 37 can be understood as an oracle of liberation: God will liberate the people of Israel from this valley of death. Indeed, prophetic literature frequently presupposes oppression and exploitation against which is spoken the liberating word of the Lord.[4]

Although the origin and social setting of the wisdom literature is disputed, careful reading of it will reveal repeated concern for social justice.[5] Proverbs 30:13-14, for instance, condemns those who, like cannibals, eat the poor, while Job 29:11-17 describes the righteous person in the language of justice. A psalm of praise like Psalm 146 becomes a liberation text when one pays close attention to God's attitude toward the weak (vv. 5-9). Indeed, the theme of justice issuing from theophany runs like a lace through the eyelets of the Psalms.

As noted in the previous chapter, apocalyptic literature is generated among those alienated from the dominant social system.[6] For instance, Revelation was written during a time when the church in Asia Minor was in a minority situation and was undergoing an unspecified persecution. In the eyes of the official culture, the church was akin to an infectious disease. Against this reality Revelation offers an alternative (liberated) view of the world. The structures of oppression, such as the great whore, are exposed for what they are and are destroyed and replaced by a new community (Revelation 21-22). Indeed, the apocalyptic interpretation of history not only calls for social change but foresees a whole new social and cosmic reality.[7]

Luke 4:16-30 is a classic liberation text. For Jesus is pictured as announcing that the liberating activity of God is conducted in behalf of the poor and that, in fact, God is moving in an aggressive way toward those that the local power structure has traditionally regarded as outcast and unclean—the poor, the sinners, the Gentiles.

The story of the Gerasene demoniac (Mark 5:1-20) can be read as little more than the report of a medical transaction. But from the perspective of liberation, the demonic possession is an oppressive reality which has perverted the structures of Legion's life. The exorcism, then, is an act of liberation which changes those structures.

While the apostle Paul does not set forth a program of social reform, liberation emphases can be found in both general and specific ways in his letters. In Christ, God has invaded the world to begin the eschatological age. A new world (or system) is released from bondage and marked by the glorious liberty of the children of God. To take a specific example, in Galatia one group in the church sees itself as superior to others. Paul indicates that in the body of Christ we are freed from the repressive separations of a former time (Galatians 3:28). The church, under the power of the Spirit, witnesses to a fundamentally new life system.

One can even sense the liberation perspective in a "theological" document like Hebrews. In that homily the goal of Christian life is to attain perfection, to follow the pioneer and perfecter of our faith to glory (heaven). In this scheme, does not "heaven" serve as a principle of social criticism? The notion of heaven stands in judgment on this earthly life and, too, carries with it the liberating promise of a renewed world "beyond caste."[8]

In making the hermeneutical movement, then, we need to identify the oppressed in our world, as well as the oppressors and the conditions that allow oppression to continue. Through what arteries of life do we feel the liberating pulse of God? How can we participate in that pulse in a concrete way? We may discover that we are one with Pharaoh and that our sumptuous way of life needs radical reorganization for us to join the impulse toward liberation.

When preaching, we want to use contemporary imagery which is as vivid and concrete as the language of the text. Indeed, one graphic image is worth pages of social analysis. Further, we need to avoid preaching the liberation message as a legalism or as only a gavel of judgment that is void of the verdict of grace.[9]

Key Questions

1. For its understanding, does this text presuppose awareness of an oppressive reality in a situation to which the text was directed?[10]
2. Can we describe how oppression was manifest in the situation to which the text was directed?

3. Did the community to which this text was directed participate in the reality of oppression as the oppressed or as the oppressor?
4. What message did this text speak:
   a. To the oppressor?
   b. To the oppressed?
5. In the contemporary world do we find oppressive situations similar to that/those of the text?
6. Does the congrègation to which the sermon will be preached participate in oppression as the oppressed or as the oppressor?
7. In the contemporary setting what is necessary for liberation to be effected?
8. Can the preacher suggest some concrete ways in which the congregation can become a part of the movement toward liberation?

Case Study: Jeremiah 22:13-17

1. For its understanding, does this text presuppose awareness of an oppressive reality in a situation to which the text was directed? A recollection of the historical setting in which Jeremiah prophesied will show why this question is to be answered yes. Judah, the locale of the prophet's ministry, was in danger of being taken over by Babylon. Jehoiakim, the monarch, was using his place of power to exploit the peasants through enforced labor and taxation in order to support his palatial habits and to buy an alliance with Egypt.[11]

2. Can we describe how oppression was manifest in the situation to which the text was directed? Jehoiakim's exploitation of the poor has led to their enforced labor and the abandonment of covenantal prescriptions which were designed to protect the poor.

3. Did the community to which this text was directed participate in the reality of oppression as the oppressed or as the oppressor? The speech is directed to the monarch and the ruling classes who supported and benefited from Jehoiakim's policies.

4. What message did this text speak:

a. To the oppressor? Jeremiah condemns Jehoiakim's policies. These policies are exemplified in the manner in which the palace was built (vv. 13-16). This demonstrates that the ruler does not "know God" (v. 16). In Jeremiah to "know God" is precisely to see that justice is performed and in particular that the rights of the poor are defended. In the context of the whole prophecy, the fall of the nation will be the ultimate result (judgment) of Jehoiakim's policies.

   b. To the oppressed? While the text does not address the oppressed directly, by reference to Jehoiakim's father, who did practice justice, the prophet implies that the situation of the poor could be rectified. In order for this to happen, Jehoiakim and the ruling class need to "know God." This might further avert the fall of Judah.

   5. *In the contemporary world do we find oppressive situations similar to that/those of the text?* The pronounced gap between the rich and the poor is well known. It is manifest between first and third worlds as well as between classes within given countries. It seems clear by now that the middle and upper classes of first-world countries and of many Third World countries do indeed occupy a place in modern society similar to that of Jehoiakim and his friends in ancient Judah.

   6. *Does the congregation to which the sermon will be preached participate in oppression as the oppressed or as the oppressor?* One must answer this question with care and sensitivity. If the sermon is preached to a white, main-line, middle- and upper-class congregation, the congregation almost certainly sits before the text with Jehoiakim and the wealthy. To be sure, we do not personally use guns and cattle prods to keep the poor in the ditches, fields, and mines; but we are complicit in a system that does not actively discourage such repressive forms of coercion. Further, our life-style is directly supported by the manipulation of the poor. In many Third World countries, farmers who could grow nourishing food on their lands, instead grow cash crops, such as sugar, to sell to "first world" markets. In turn, they use the cash to buy, from the first world, food which is less nutritious than they could grow. In addition, first-world advertisers now direct their promotional activities to the most remote communities to sell everything from baby formula to electric utensils. Sales, of course, are profits, and profits keep stockholders

happy and investing. At the same time though, we need to remember that each congregation contains persons at different levels of economic, social, and political power, many of whom (even in the first world) are victims of the manipulation of others. We also need to remember that few of the very powerful are intentionally cruel.

7. *In the contemporary setting what is necessary for liberation to be effected?* Justice requires an equitable distribution of resources and a fair sharing of power. It is difficult to see how this can happen without fundamental changes in first-world values and practices. Without a systemic change, wealth will continue to flow into the first world with the resultant degradation of the poor.

8. *Can the preacher suggest some concrete ways in which the congregation can become a part of the movement toward liberation?* The text itself uses images of Jehoiakim's life-style to exemplify his oppressive practices. Perhaps the preacher can relate the lifestyle of the members of the congregation to the exploitation of the poor. For example, every time a person reaches for a piece of aluminum foil, the aluminum industry is rewarded for buying the farmland of Haitians for a pittance and sending the former landowners to live in urban slums in filth and poverty. At a basic and symbolic level, we can give up some things. At least this would dramatize our commitment to justice. Beyond that, we can participate in measures to influence corporate behavior (and our national government's behavior) in Third World countries by joining boycotts and withdrawing funds from banks which make loans to repressive governments. We can identify with movements which work actively and explicitly for justice.

Suggestions for Further Reading

The literature of liberation theology is vast but can be grouped according to three closely related sub-categories: (1) from the perspective of the Third World—Africa, Asia and Latin America; (2) from the perspective of North American blacks; and (3) from the perspective of women. General introductions include Catherine G. and Justo L. Gonzalez, *Liberation Preaching: The Pulpit and the Oppressed* (Nashville: Abingdon Press, 1980); Alvin C. Porteous, *Preaching to Suburban Captives* (Valley Forge: Judson Press, 1979);

Robert M. Brown, *Theology in a New Key: Responding to Liberation Themes* (Philadelphia: The Westminster Press, 1978); James H. Cone, *My Soul Looks Back* (Nashville: Abingdon Press, 1982); William K. McElvaney, *Good News Is Bad News Is Good News* (Maryknoll: Orbis Books, 1980).

Third World liberation theology is not of a single mind. Representative works include Jose M. Bonino, *Doing Theology in a Revolutionary Situation,* ed. William H. Lazareth (Philadelphia: Fortress Press, 1975); Gustavo Gutierrez, *A Theology of Liberation,* trans. Caridad Inda, Sr., and John Eagleson (Maryknoll: Orbis Books, 1973); J. Severino Croatto, *Exodus: A Hermeneutics of Freedom* (Maryknoll: Orbis Books, 1981); Jose P. Miranda, *Marx and the Bible: A Critique of the Philosophy of Oppression,* trans. John Eagleson (Maryknoll: Orbis Books, 1974) and *Being and the Messiah: The Message of St. John* (Maryknoll: Orbis Books, 1977); Choan-Seng Song, *Third-Eye Theology: Theology in Formation in Asian Settings* (Maryknoll: Orbis Books, 1979); John S. Pobee, *Toward an African Theology* (Nashville: Abingdon Press, 1979); *African Theology en Route: Papers from the Pan-African Conference of Third World Theologians, December 17-23, 1977,* ed. Kofi Appiah-Kubi and Sergio Torres (Maryknoll: Orbis Books, 1978).

A leading black theologian is James H. Cone, author of *God of the Oppressed* (New York: The Seabury Press, Inc., 1975) and *A Black Theology of Liberation* (Philadelphia: J. B. Lippincott Co., 1970). A massive anthology, edited by Gayraud S. Wilmore and James H. Cone, is *Black Theology: A Documentary History, 1966-1979* (Maryknoll: Orbis Books, 1979). Other contributions (not necessarily of the same mind as Cone) include: Gayraud Wilmore, *Black Religion and Black Radicalism* (New York: Doubleday Publishing Co., 1972); J. Deotis Roberts, *Roots of a Black Future: Family and Church* (Philadelphia: The Westminster Press, 1980); and Major J. Jones, *Christian Ethics for Black Theology* (Nashville: Abingdon Press, 1974).

Liberation theology from the perspective of women may enfold the greatest variation of viewpoint of any of the wings of liberation thought. Some works of interest include Sheila D. Collins, *A Dif-*

ferent Heaven and Earth (Valley Forge: Judson Press, 1974); Mary
Daly, *Beyond God the Father: Toward a Philosophy of Women's
Liberation* (Boston: Beacon Press, 1973) and *Gyn-Ecology: The
Metaethics of Radical Feminism* (Boston: Beacon Press, 1979); Letty
M. Russell, *Human Liberation in a Feminist Perspective: A Theology*
(Philadelphia: The Westminster Press, 1974) and *The Liberating
Word: A Guide to Non-Sexist Interpretation of the Bible,* ed. Letty
M. Russell (Philadelphia: The Westminster Press, 1976); *Language
About God in Liturgy and Scripture,* ed. Barbara Withers (Phila-
delphia: Geneva, 1980); Virginia R. Mollenkott, *Women, Men and
the Bible* (Nashville: Abingdon Press, 1977) and the many writings
of Rosemary R. Ruether, especially *New Woman-New Earth: Sexist
Ideologies and Human Liberation* (New York; The Seabury Press,
1978).

10

Interpreting a Biblical Text As a Work of Art

Over the past thirty years, interest has increased in the relationship between religion and the arts. A significant and growing body of literature stresses the importance of the arts in the formation and expression of religious experience. Careful attention is given to the life of the congregation as a context for expressive media such as drama, dance, symbolic gesture and movement, the fabric arts, architecture, poetry. Preaching itself is again being spoken of as an art. In this chapter I suggest that we can understand parts of the Bible in somewhat the same way that we understand art and that the sermon can assume some of the characteristics of art.

Art As Representation of Feeling[1]

Basic to understanding parts of the Bible as art is understanding art itself. Art is the creation of representations of human feeling.[2] Basic then to understanding art is understanding human feelings and how they are represented in art.

In ordinary conversation when we speak of "feeling," we have reference to physical or emotional states. "How are you feeling today?" "I feel angry at the professor for giving me that grade after I practically wore the letters off the keys of the typewriter preparing it.'' While the philosophy of art includes the physical and emotional in its understanding of feeling, it includes much more.

A feeling is whatever is felt, from physical sensation to complicated emotions to the tensions generated by intellectual life.[3] I feel one way when boiling water from the tea kettle splashes on my hand and another way when I stand in the midnight darkness in my bare feet and hear over the phone that my father has died and still another way when an idea surges through my mind like electricity. I may not be able fully to describe such feelings in conventional language, but I *know* them as surely as I know the multiplication tables.

Thus, we may speak of two realms of knowledge. The more familiar realm is that of facts and ideas. I know the multiplication tables, the order of the books of the Bible, the principles of the Constitution of the United States, the rules of a football game, and the guidelines on how to make an ethically responsible decision on the question of the church's position on a contemporary social question. The other realm is the realm of feeling. Of course, in a whole self or community, the two types of knowledge are not mutually exclusive but are integrated so that head and heart, rational thought and intuitive feeling, are engaged in complementary ways.

Conventional thought and knowledge can be expressed through the conventional use of language and symbolism, but in our culture, the chief interpreter of the life of feeling is the artist.

That artist has an awareness within the life of feeling, an intuitive experience. The artist then makes a representation of this feeling in another medium, for example, a musical composition, a sculpture, a painting, a dance. The representation is not a blueprint but is an embodiment, an incarnation. A painting is not so much a picture of the subject of the painting as it is an interpretation of the artist's feeling.

In addition to intentionally created works of art, the intuitive life can be expressed unintentionally and spontaneously. Dream images, for instance, seem to rise from the life of feeling.[4] And according to Susanne Langer's reconstruction of the rise of human consciousness, the earliest forms of human expression—dance and song—were representations of the inner life. Around the campfire, the dancer acted out his or her intuitive understanding of the meaning of life.[5]

The intuitive also comes to expression in the form of myth, which can be understood as a representation of the feeling of a person or a community of what it is like to be in the world. Through the motif of narrative and personification the myth explains the various inter-relationships of nature and humankind as well as of human beings with one another.[6] The earliest form of language to make its way into human expression was narrative: the story was (and is) a way of locating the self and the community amidst the great cosmic realities.[7]

A well-written or spoken piece can add to our reservoir of personal and communal history by letting us participate in an event (past, present, future) in our imaginations. A good language artist will include all the detail which is necessary for apprehension and will omit the distracting details that often accompany real-life events (such as the lawn mower roaring outside the window or a constant nasal drip). A good work is shaped economically but fully. There-fore, being engaged by a good poem, a short story, a drama, or a novel can be better than being present at an actual event.

An important advantage of the written arts is their ability to integrate the rational and the logical with the intuitive and the feeling more easily than other media. An integrated piece can speak to the whole self in a way that logical argumentation by itself cannot. On the other hand, those aspects of discursive reasoning which are voiced in a written piece can elevate the significance of intuitive experience and place it in a conscious framework of meaning.

When the viewer (or listener or reader) gives himself or herself to the artwork in the appropriate way, something of the same feeling is stirred in the viewer as was stirring in the artist. However, because the inner life of each person is unique, that which is represented in the art symbol is not completely duplicated in the viewer. The response of the viewer is not a photocopy of the feeling of the artist. It is more like an interpretation within the viewer's own life. Indeed, *the experience of viewing (or listening or reading) is itself a large part of the meaning of the piece.* That is, what I *feel* as I watch, listen, or read is a major part of the "message" of the work.

I stand before Monet's "Water Lilies" and look. I listen as the choir sings DuBois' "Seven Last Words." In my imagination, I live John Irving's *The World According to Garp;* its tensions become my tensions and Garp's world is added to my own reservoir of experience.

Biblical Text As Representation of Feeling

Many biblical texts are similar to works of art in the general sense that they use language to embody the life of feeling. Further, many biblical texts, formed in response to social, economic, political, and religious tension, integrate the rational/logical/analytical with the intuitive/feeling. In the ancient setting, the listener or reader received not only a logical theological statement but also a feeling: the text spoke to the whole self, to the heart as well as to the head.

Because biblical texts are cast in language and imagery from another time and culture, they often seem strange and alien to us. The evocative power of a text may be diminished to the point that our response to the text may be puzzlement: "What in the name of heaven is that all about?"

Texts are culturally conditioned and to enter the world of the text, we need to become acculturated. I take this to be a major purpose of exegesis—to let us enter the world of the text on its own terms. However, much traditional exegesis is one-dimensional. It focuses on the rational element in the text and attempts to answer questions like "What did this text mean in its ancient context?" Even synchronic exegesis tends to be highly analytical and to discuss the text as if it were an inert object of research.

 To interpret a text as a representation of feeling is to recover the associations of feelings which the early listeners or readers would have experienced with the language and imagery of the text. I find it helpful to ask these questions: What feelings come to expression in this text? and What feelings are evoked by this text?

One must be careful not to answer these questions in such a way that the answers let the air out of the text and flatten it. If I say, "I love my wife," that statement can mean anything from a response to being playfully pushed into a pile of fall leaves to gratitude for something she has done for me to a driving sexual urge.

Of course, the interpretation of a text from the perspective of a work of art cannot account for the whole understanding of a text. But it can bring to light some neglected dimensions of meaning.

In Genesis 22, we read of Abraham taking Isaac up the mountain for sacrifice. At one point in the history of the narrative, some of Israel's neighbors may have practiced human sacrifice. The firstborn son of the family was sacrificed to a god. What could it feel like to serve such a god? Perhaps the story of Abraham and Isaac atop the mountain is a picture of what it means to serve the God of the Hebrews. The same God who demands the boy graciously provides the ram. Serving this God is like a man taking his only child up the mountain—and both of them coming down smelling of charred lamb.[8]

The book of Leviticus is widely regarded as a "handbook" for the operation of the cult. Leviticus 16 describes a ritual for atonement for sin. What feeling would cause such a text to be written? Beneath the prescriptive language, perhaps, is the feeling of uncleanness caused by sin and the longing for that feeling to be relieved.

In Hosea 11, we have the famous description of God's relationship to Israel in which God is described by the use of traditional feminine imagery. God nurtures Israel in the same way that a mother nurtures her child. Thus, when Hosea uses the image of the mother-child relationship, the image expresses and evokes the feeling of that human relationship and transfers it to God.

The subject of the parable of the ten maidens (Matthew 25:1-12) is the royal rule of God. That rule is likened to a wedding feast and thus evokes the full range of associations which accompany a Near Eastern wedding, but the royal rule of God is delayed, so the church is in a position like that of the maidens who are waiting for the feast. To say "the church is waiting for the royal rule of God to come in its fullness" is an accurate but insufficient summary of the parable. The image of the women waiting outside the door for the bridegroom creates a world of intuitive associations.

The Hellenistic world in which the hymn of Colossians 1:15-20 came to expression was marked by the belief that life was under the control of fate, a blind force that ruled with an inexorable and unpredictable hand. The polytheism of that world was, in part, an attempt to overcome the feeling of being trapped. Perhaps by manipulating the gods, one could gain a measure of favor and freedom. In this world, the Christ hymn describes the different experience of the church: in place of the blind contradictions of life, the church experiences reconciliation and peace. The agency through which this reconciliation is mediated is the fellowship of the church.

In exegesis we may want to give special attention to particular words or metaphors, even in texts which are not obviously infused with feeling. For a metaphor, no matter how small, is not just a decorative ornament. It embraces the movement of consciousness itself, and that movement is an important part of the meaning of the piece.[9] Thus, the experience of hearing or reading a metaphor touches the life of feeling.

The psalmist prays, "Wash me thoroughly from my iniquity . . ." (Psalm 51:2). The metaphor "wash me" indicates the psalmist's feeling about the effect of sin in life: it makes one feel unclean, dirty, in need of cleansing as the body is in need of a bath after a day in the barnyard.

Paul says, "We know that the whole creation has been groaning in travail together until now . . ." (Romans 8:22). The creation is not literally a pregnant woman about to give birth, but that figure of speech evokes a deeply intuitive response. For to be in the creation is to feel like a panting, white-knuckled woman bearing down on the bed as a contraction tightens like a steel band around her belly.

Sermon As Representation of Feeling

The philosophy of art suggests that the purpose of a sermon is not to explain the feeling embodied in a text, but to create that feeling for the modern congregation through the medium of the sermon. We can thus speak of the sermon as a representation of feeling much like a work of art.

As the text is a world into which the reader or listener enters, so the sermon can create a world into which the congregation can enter and which can touch the congregation in intuitive as well as in rational ways. The shape, size, and content of the sermonic world will be determined by the text.

Because we are often estranged from the imagery of the text, the preacher may want to use, in today's setting, contemporary language and imagery which have evocative power equal in strength to that of the language and imagery of the text in its setting. Just as an important purpose of exegesis is to place the preacher in a position to feel the intuitive power of the text, so a purpose of the sermon is to place the congregation in a position to be stirred by the text in ways akin to those of the listeners of the world of biblical times.

This is the point at which the preacher's sensitivity to the text *and* to the life of his or her congregation and community becomes critical; for in ways unknown to scholars in New Haven, Chicago, or Berkeley, each congregation has associations and ideas which arise uniquely from its life—the knowing smiles which accompany the mention of a particular curmudgeon, the smell at the bottom of the stairs, the not-so-funny jokes about the string of missile silos buried in the cornfields on the edge of town. The irreplaceable role of the local preacher is to use symbols, images, and associations from the local community and culture through which the congregation can enter the world of the text.

What will evoke an intuitive response similar to the feeling conveyed by the story of Abraham and Isaac? How do we express the feeling of uncleanness in Leviticus 16? A contemporary wedding reception with its stiff reception line, tasteless cake, and innocuous punch hardly calls forth the feeling of a wedding feast like the one in Matthew 25. However, we do wait for something with a similar sense of anticipation and association. In what ways do we experience the reconciliation pictured in the Christ hymn of Colossians? Do we experience it in the fellowship of the church, with its hassles over the church kitchen? If not in the church, what image does arouse the feeling of fellowship?

Of course not all sermons can be (or should be) works of art of the kind described in this chapter, but nearly all sermons will contain moments and metaphors which represent the life of feeling. Certainly, all sermons can profit from the artist's economy of style and reluctance to clutter the piece with unnecessary embroidery. In the case of the sermon, the unnecessary material is words. In order to clarify and reinforce, we sometimes add word upon word until life-giving ideas are so weighted down that they sink below the waterline of the listener's awareness.

This is especially true in the use of stories and as the sermon draws to a close. I seldom hear a story which is allowed to stand on its own feet, as are short stories, novels and the stories of the Bible. A well-told story, like the incident of Abraham going up the mountain with Isaac, carries its own message. To explain it, much more to draw out a moral, is to violate the integrity of the story and to limit the listener's perception of the story to the size of one's own comment. Finally, the end of the sermon which should be pungent and graceful, is sometimes like an old field over which the plow has crossed for too many seasons. The soil, once loamy and fertile, grows thin and erodes. At the conclusion of the sermon, I find that less is usually more.

Key Questions

1. What feeling is expressed in this text?
2. How can that feeling be expressed adequately in a sermon?

Case Study: Isaiah 6:1-8

1. What feeling is expressed in this text? In order to recover the feeling embodied in the text, I look carefully at the images and determine their associations and evocations.[10] The Lord on a throne is "high and lifted up." The seraphim, mentioned only here in canonical Jewish literature, are apparently winged celestial beings who serve the Lord and who sing of the holiness and glory of the Lord. To see the seraphim (whose name means something like "burning ones") and to hear the song is to know that one is in the presence of the Lord.

The effect of that presence is further described in the image of the foundations of the thresholds shaking. The coming of God is like an earthquake which shakes the foundations of the created order.

Fire and smoke recall other instances of the manifestation of the

Lord. Indeed, fire is such a recurring feature of theophany that we might say that to be in the presence of the Lord is like being in the presence of fire.

Seraphim. Fire. Smoke. The shaking of the foundations. That is what it is like to be in the presence of the Lord.

Isaiah's response to such a powerful vision could be my own. "Woe is me!" Rudolf Otto is right: the *mysterium tremendum* is both fascinating and frightening; we are attracted and we are afraid.

What the experience of awe and majesty does is not for its own sake. The ecstasy overflows into ministry and mission. "Here am I! Send me." Ecstasy turned only inward can curdle. And ministry without a power base can result in ethically correct actions but sterile and even self-righteous ministers. On the way to a peace march, I was once shoved out of the way by an impatient seminary student wearing a tee-shirt on which was stenciled "All We Are Saying Is Give Peace a Chance."

2. How can that feeling be expressed adequately in a sermon? One can talk *about* the awe which this passage both embodies and induces. But one of the goals of a sermon on the text is to set the congregation trembling, to help the congregation experience what it is like to see the Lord "high and lifted up."

When have I been aware of such a powerful presence? When have I had an experience that made me tremble so much that I wanted to cry out?

We were hiking in the Sangre de Cristo Mountains in New Mexico when an afternoon thunderstorm blew up in the time it takes to get a poncho out of the backpack. Underneath a rock overhang I sat as the wind filled the canyon as though it were a balloon about to burst. Thunder shook my tin camping gear. Hail-sized raindrops splashed onto my dusty boots. Lightning splintered a tree an arm's length away. Awesome.

I remember my reaction the first time I watched a film clip of a nuclear blast: "My God!" Sometimes a symphony builds to a crescendo which leaves my heart in my mouth. Arms linked in the streets at dusk, half a million voices, all singing, "All we are saying is give peace a chance. . . ."

The preacher will want to make a connection between the experience of the holy and ministry. Indeed, the awareness of the holy can commission us for ministry. If I have had a glimpse of what it is like to be in the presence of the Holy One of Israel, what Caesar need I fear?

Suggestions for Further Reading

A basic introduction to the relationship of art and religious life is G. van der Leeuw, *Sacred and Profane Beauty* (New York: Holt, Rinehart & Winston, 1963). More general but related works are his *Religion in Essence and Manifestation,* (New York: Harper & Row Publishers, Inc., 1963), two vols.; and Rudolf Otto, *The Idea of the Holy,* trans. John W. Harvey (New York: Oxford University Press, Inc., 1958). A basic theological understanding of the same is that of Paul Tillich, especially *Theology of Culture,* ed. Robert C. Kimball (New York: Oxford University Press, Inc., 1959). Many Christian interpreters either follow Tillich's lead or react against him.

For the purpose of simplicity, in this chapter I have relied on only one philosophy of art, that of Susanne K. Langer. Among her basic works are *Philosophy in a New Key,* (New York: The New American Library, Inc., 1959); *Feeling and Form* (New York: Charles Scribner's Sons, 1953); *Problems of Art* (New York: Charles Scribner's Sons, 1957); *Philosophical Sketches* (Baltimore: The Johns Hopkins University Press, 1962); *Mind: An Essay on Human Feeling,* three vols. (Baltimore: The Johns Hopkins University Press, 1967, 1972, 1983). A similar line of argument is found in the difficult writings of Ernst Cassirer. This, of course, is only one way in which the nature of artistic expression may be understood. See Monroe C. Beardsley, *Aesthetics from Classical Greece to the Present: A Short History* (Tuscaloosa: University of Alabama Press, 1975) as well as any number of anthologies, for example, *Aesthetics,* ed. Jerome Stolnitz (New York: Macmillan, Inc., 1965).

A pioneer interpreter of the relationship between artistic expression and biblical study is Amos N. Wilder (though he does not adopt the particular perspective I have articulated). Among his important works are *Early Christian Rhetoric: The Language of the Gospel* (Cambridge: Harvard University Press, 1971); *Theopoetic: Theology and the Religious Imagination* (Philadelphia: Fortress Press, 1976) and *Jesus' Parables and the War of Myths: Essays on Imagination in the Scriptures* (Philadelphia: Fortress Press, 1982). Another biblical scholar with remarkable sensitivity to the aesthetic dimension of the text is Samuel Terrien, especially in his summa *The Elusive Presence: Toward a New Biblical Theology* (New York: Harper & Row Publishers, Inc., 1978). An older work is Geraint V. Jones, *The Art and Truth of the Parables* (London: SPCK, 1964).

An extraordinary book which contributes to this discussion indirectly is Frederick Buechner, *Telling the Truth: The Gospel As Tragedy, Comedy, and Fairy Tale* (New York: Harper & Row Publishers, Inc., 1977). Attention is given to similar themes by Charles Rice, *Interpretation and Imagination: The Preacher and Contemporary Literature* (Philadelphia: Fortress Press, 1970) and the work of Fred B. Craddock, especially *Overhearing the Gospel* (Nashville: Abingdon Press, 1978) and *As One Without Authority,* 3rd ed. (Nashville: Abingdon Press, 1979).

while others have been wanting

11

Canonical Criticism: The Problem of Contemporary Authority

A visit to the sewing room will nearly always reveal a menagerie of the bits and pieces of fabric, pattern, and thread of a garment in the process of being made. Some of the pieces of the pattern have been pinned on large swaths of cloth and are awaiting the scissors while others have been carefully cut and now sit in a wicker basket by the sewing machine, ready to be joined to a half-finished liturgical vestment. In the corner are several different colors and designs laid next to each other to see which will go together.

While such discovery is fascinating, when the time comes for me to wear the vestment while leading worship, I am not nearly as interested in how the pieces were laid out in the sewing room, or in how far the operator of the sewing machine had to twist and turn in order to get them under the needle of the sewing machine, as I am in how the finished piece fits and in its effect in the service of worship. The final form and quality of the garment is my most important concern. Will the individual panels and seams and tucks come together to be an adequate symbol for worship? Will it fit snugly enough or will it bind and chafe?

In something of the same way, canonical criticism is primarily interested in the final form of the text.[1] While the history of a text is fascinating and important, the canonical critic is finally drawn to the fully developed form of the text, for that form has been shaped by the religious community in order to function as canon—authority—for the church. The important canonical question is that of how the text comes to be authoritative in the life of the people of God today. Thus, in a way quite different from other critical disciplines, canonical criticism deals with contemporary significance.

The Search for the Significance of the Bible

Canonical criticism, whose beginnings date only to the late 1960s, is associated principally with the work of Brevard Childs and James Sanders. Childs traces the reasons for its appearance in his book *Biblical Theology in Crisis*.[2] Following World War II biblical studies rallied around a theological approach to the interpretation of the Bible which is commonly called the biblical theology movement. The movement began as a reaction against sterile, purely historical means of biblical interpretation. Although the contributors to this movement made unique contributions, their common emphasis was on rediscovering the theological vitality of the Bible.

According to Childs they shared key elements: (1) the unity (with diversity) of the whole Bible; (2) historical acts as the means by which revelation comes; and (3) a distinct biblical perspective on faith and life which could be distinguished from the perspectives of the neighbors of Israel and the church.[3] In the late 1950s and early 1960s, these taproots were cut at the base. The unity of the Bible as described by the biblical theology movement was shown to be an artificial construct which overlooked fundamental differences among texts. More sophisticated analyses of history demonstrated the difficulty of speaking of God acting in history. The distinct biblical perspective was eroded by increasing attention to the similarities between the thinking of the biblical peoples and their neighbors.[4]

While consensus about the interpretation of the Bible eroded, the Bible itself remained at the center of the life of the people of God. What role should the Bible play? What is the relationship between the Bible and preaching and teaching? Canonical criticism addresses such questions.

Canonical criticism does not regard the authority of the Bible in a dogmatic or ahistorical way. The important clue to canonical criticism is the observation of the process by which the ancient communities of faith found the documents we now call canonical to shape their identity and behavior. That process suggests a paradigm for ways in which the canon can become authoritative for us.

Ancient communities of faith were much like our own. On one hand they had inherited a body of tradition from the past. On the other hand, they lived in particular historical moments, fraught with their own tensions and often quite removed from the situation(s) which gave rise to the inherited tradition. What does a tradition several hundred years removed say to the living community?

What difference does the escapade of the deception of Isaac make when we have been exiled? What is the relevance of sacrifice when the temple has been destroyed? How shall a struggling church interpret traditional Jewish literature in light of the resurrection of Jesus?

After extensive analysis of the process by which our ancestors in Israel and in the church came to answer such questions, canonical critics conclude that the canon is both stable and adaptable. It is stable in that the contents have been fixed. The boundary lines have resisted those who would resurvey the terrain with transits of narrower theological sight lines. It is adaptable in that it contains within it the power, depth and breadth to address each generation afresh with a word appropriate to the new context.

An important factor in the adaptability of the canon is its pluralism.[5] Of course the Bible is monotheistic, that is, concerned with the one sovereign God. But the divine dealings with the human family are expressed in a variety of ways, some of which flatly contradict each other. Isaiah 2:1-4 and Micah 4:1-3, loved by the peace movements of history, speak of the beating of swords into plowshares. Yet Joel 3:10 advises preparation for war by beating plowshares into swords. Mark 13 seems to picture the apocalyptic moment as about to happen, whereas 2 Peter 3 explains the delay by saying with Psalm 90:4, ". . . with the Lord one day is as a thousand years. . . ."

Such pluralism causes no weeping and gnashing of teeth among canonical critics. Instead, they rejoice in the theological statement made by pluralism: the word of God is always specific and directed to the needs of particular people at particular moments in history. Pluralism testifies to the sovereign freedom of God who is not the captive of a set of systematically related propositions. God cannot be put into a box. Indeed, the pluralism of the canon calls into question any effort on our part to make absolute any agenda. If a single point of view, such as social justice or the charismatic experience becomes *the* lens through which the Bible is read, the canon contains its own important correctives.

Unity is not to be found in the Bible (as in the biblical theology movement) but in God, who has the sovereign freedom even to justify the ungodly. Like the prophet John who fell down before the angel, we sometimes worship the Bible and need to hear the admonition, ". . . Worship God" (Revelation 22:9).

Two Functions of Canon

Texts arose to meet the needs of the community at given moments in history. The two needs which the canon most commonly addressed in the biblical period were confirmation and challenge.[6] These are the two main functions of the canon in the church today.

The canon provides a word of confirmation to the community which is in danger of losing its sense of identity and which may even be doubting the reality of the promises of God.[7] This community needs pastoral support. "You are my people." The canon speaks a word of prophetic challenge to the community which has strayed from its calling and mission and which needs to be recalled to its true ministry. Often such a community believes that it is elect and blessed but is not living up to what that means.

At the time of Josiah, when national identity was being reconstituted, 2 Samuel 7 was understood as confirmation of Josianic rule. At the time of the Exile, the morale of the people paralleled the physical condition of the temple—in ruins. In that setting the story of the Exodus came as a source of confirmation. The Exodus is a paradigm of what God will do for those in exile.[8] A community returned from exile is unable to refocus its energy and mission and is given the books of Ezra and Nehemiah with their emphasis on obedience as the proper fulfillment of community life.[9] A religious community that has been banned from the synagogue understands its true identity in a traditional image of the people of God; they are a true "sheepfold" (John 10).

In the time of Hosea, the Northern Kingdom had no doubt about its election, but the prophet graphically challenges that security with the image of the harlot. To a strict community that is having trouble absorbing Gentile converts, the Book of Ruth challenges the people to remember that the heroine herself was a Moabite. To a congregation of Jewish Christians whose inner life is vitriolic, Matthew 18 is a challenge to recover the meaning of forgiveness. In a church which has forgotten the meaning of community, Acts 2-5 holds forth a vision toward which the community is challenged to move.

Almost any text can be read as both affirmation and prophetic challenge. Psalm 23, which in our era almost always performs a pastoral function (especially at the time of death), can also be read as a prophetic challenge. Of course "The Lord is my shepherd," but in the modern era we turn to other shepherds. The corporation is my shepherd, and as a rising young executive, where they lead me, I will follow. The psalm thus challenges our notion of shepherd. Paul opens Romans 5 with "Therefore, since we are justified by faith, we have peace with God. . . ." To those whose daily experience is akin to living in a live mine field, the words offer pastoral support: you can have peace. But to others, who justify their (our) lives on the basis of vocational, academic, economic, social, or familial achievements, the apostle makes a prophetic challenge: we are justified by *faith*.

For preaching, the fundamental canonical task is to assess the need of the congregation. Does the congregation need pastoral support or prophetic challenge? The analysis of the congregation will determine whether one preaches in the mode of confirmation or of challenge.[10]

According to Childs, we must come to grips with the final form of the canon because it alone "bears witness to the full history of revelation."[11] Now canonical criticism does not mean that we equate the meaning of the text to what was spoken to the final historical situation in which the text was given its canonical meaning. Rather, we attempt to identify the *abiding theological significance* of the text for generations subsequent to that in which the text was given its final form.

Take the famous words of the Lord, quoted by Amos, "Let justice roll down like waters, and righteousness like an everflowing stream" (5:24). From a strictly historical viewpoint, the words call for the reform of Israel; but from the canonical viewpoint, the text shows that righteousness and justice are integral standards for the life of the people of God.[12] Ephesians 2 describes the unity in Christ of the uncircumcised and the circumcised. While that is hardly a problem for today's church, the abiding significance of the text may be its affirmation that in Christ (in the church) the fundamental differences between people ("the dividing walls of hostility") have been replaced by unity in relationship, described by the author as "one new person in place of the two."

Once the assessment is made, Sanders offers a suggestion for sermon preparation: identify with the person or group in the text (or in the setting to which the text was spoken). This will allow the text to speak the appropriate word of confirmation or challenge. "In order to hear this text appropriately, with whom do I identify?" Sanders provides a theological plumb line by which to gauge the adequacy of our interpretation. "Whenever our reading of a biblical passage makes us feel self-righteous, we can be confident we have misread it."[13] On the other hand, our sense of discomfort with the passage may be in direct proportion to the accuracy of our reading. Given the cultural situation of the main-line church, comfortable and powerful, Sanders argues that prophetic challenge will more often than not be the fitting mode in which to read the text.[14]

Thus, to grasp the full canonical thrust of the text, we will not ordinarily identify with the hero or heroine (e.g. Jeremiah, Joanna, Jesus, John) but with those who are in need of help or correction. I am not Moses, but one of those murmuring in the wilderness. I am not the shepherd looking for the lost sheep, but I am the sheep. I am not Paul standing before Festus, but I am the governor who blurts out, "Paul, you are mad!" I read the letters of John not as the writer, but as those who desperately need to hear the words, "Beloved, let us love one another."

An example so pointed that it appears in nearly all of Sanders's writings is the sermon of Jesus at Nazareth (Luke 4:16-30). If we identify with Jesus, we will be led to feelings of anger at the respectable church crowd that tried to lynch Jesus. On the other hand, if we identify with the crowd, then we feel the offense which Jesus caused by speaking of God going to those who were outside the chosen community. What? "Elijah's sustaining and being sustained by a Black Muslim, I mean a Phoenician widow, and Elisha's healing a commie. . . ."[15]

A practical matter for sermon preparation is the relationship of texts to each other. A fundamental rule of canonical criticism is to honor the integrity of each text. That is, the text is to be interpreted in its own light rather than in harmony with other texts that may present different perspectives.

Biblical messages were addressed to the covenant community and seldom to the world at large. The speaker, even an angry Moses or a strident Paul, understood himself or herself as part of the covenant community and, thus, also under the grace and judgment of the word. As preachers, we too sit with the congregation under the text whether it be supportive or prophetic. A true canonical preacher does not let the height of the pulpit deceive him or her into thinking that the preaching office places one above the congregation. Indeed, as one prepares the sermon, it might be healthy to imagine oneself sitting in a pew about halfway back.

Key Questions

1. What was the function of this text in the community to which it was addressed? (Pastoral support? Prophetic challenge?)
2. What is the theological thrust of the passage which is important to the religious community beyond the situation to which the text was directed?
3. As I consider the situation of my congregation, are we in need of hearing the text as pastoral support or as prophetic challenge?

4. In order to hear this text appropriately, with whom do we identify?

Case Study: Haggai 1:1-10

1. What was the function of this text in the community to which it was addressed? (Pastoral support? Prophetic challenge?) Haggai was directed to those who had returned from the Exile to Jerusalem. Apparently those who returned dedicated themselves not to rebuilding the temple (one of the central symbols of Judaism) but to making themselves secure. They dwelt in ''paneled houses'' while the temple lay in ruins (Haggai 1:4). Despite their efforts, the land was in drought and the economy had collapsed. The one ''. . . who earns wages earns wages to put them into a bag with holes'' (1:6). Self-centered efforts, void of worship and its ethical resultant, have not brought security.

Haggai is clear about the reason for these decrepit conditions. The people have failed to rebuild the temple. The individuals have been self-absorbed in their own businesses while the Lord's business went unattended, and that meant debt and deficit for the whole community. Thus, Haggai's word is one of prophetic challenge. Like a rider's heels dug into the horse, it is intended to spur the community into action.[16]

2. What is the theological thrust of the passage which is important to the religious community beyond the situation to which the text was directed? Because of its emphasis on the temple, the text has had an honored place in building campaigns, but the church building hardly has the strength of symbol for us that the temple had in the world of Haggai. In any case, one can argue that in light of the world hunger situation, the critical issues of development in the Third World, and related human phenomena, lavish expenditures for bricks and boards would have exactly the opposite effect on the religious community today that the building of the temple would have had in the time of Haggai. Such expenditure might only reinforce the self-absorption of the modern church.

The deeper theological claim is that the business of the Lord, that is, covenant fidelity in worship and ethics, is the central business of the church. Just as the temple was a place where the glory of

God appeared, so that glory can be manifest when and where we take shovel in hand.

3. As I consider the situation of my congregation, are we in need of hearing this text as pastoral support or as prophetic challenge? At the level of the individual, our culture is certainly centered in self-preservation and self-enhancement, symbolized perhaps, by the video-game arcade. The arcade is a self-enclosed, private technological world. Its only purpose is entertainment and ego satisfaction.

Most main-line congregations already have worship facilities that would make Haggai think that the eschatological age has come. In fact, keeping the floors polished, the flowers in the chancel, and refurnishing the downstairs restroom (in colors approved by the all-church decorating committee) can become the meaning of ministry. Even given the fact that fine facilities and fine programs project a positive public image and allow us to bring our best to the Lord, whenever topics of self-interest become disproportionate in board meetings and on the parking lot, we may need to hear these words as a prophetic challenge. For instance, what is the Lord's business for our church today?

4. In order to hear this text appropriately, with whom do we identify? Clearly we are the workers to whom the text was addressed. We live in paneled houses, and in our own way, we never have enough. Like the people of old, we need to make the connection between mission and fulfillment. What temples should we be building?

Suggestions for Further Reading

Two scholars, Brevard Childs and James Sanders, provide the most important literature of canonical criticism. Because they have published only a few books, I list an unusual number of articles.

Brevard S. Childs describes the situation which led to the emergence of canonical criticism in his *Biblical Theology in Crisis* (Philadelphia: The Westminster Press, 1970). He has also produced a major commentary from the canonical perspective, *The Book of Exodus: A Critical, Theological Commentary* (Philadelphia: The Westminster Press, 1974). The same prolific author has written a full-scale introductory work from this stance: *Introduction to the*

Old Testament As Scripture (Philadelphia: Fortress Press, 1979). Among his important articles are "The Exegetical Significance of the Canon for the Study of the Old Testament," *Supplements to Vetus Testamentum* 29 (1978), pp. 66-80; "Response to Reviewers," *Journal for the Study of the Old Testament* 16 (1980), pp. 52-60.

James A. Sanders, who has a more existential orientation than Childs, often writes in a way that is more directly homiletically accessible than Childs. An overview of his perspective is *Torah and Canon* (Philadelphia: Fortress Press, 1972). An intriguing book of sermons in the canonical mode with a significant introduction is *God Has a Story Too: Biblical Sermons in Context* (Philadelphia: Fortress Press, 1979). A pivotal article is "Adaptable for Life: The Nature and Function of Canon," *Magnalia Dei*, ed. F. Cross, W. Lemke, P. Miller (Garden City: Doubleday Publishing Co., Inc., 1976), pp. 531-560. Other articles include "Hermeneutics," *The Interpreter's Dictionary of the Bible: Supplementary Volume*, Keith R. Crim, editor (Nashville: Abingdon Press, 1976), pp. 402-407; "Biblical Criticism and the Bible as Canon," *Union Seminary Quarterly Review* 32 (1977), pp. 157-165; "Canonical Context and Canonical Criticism," *Horizons in Biblical Theology* 2 (1980), pp. 173-197.

Journals which have recently devoted whole issues to canonical criticism include *Horizons in Biblical Theology* 2 (1980), *Journal for the Study of the Old Testament* 16 (1980). For other works that discuss this perspective see *Canon and Authority: Essays in Old Testament Religion and Theology*, ed. George W. Coates and Burke O. Long (Philadelphia: Fortress Press, 1977) and Joseph Blenkinsopp, *Prophecy and Canon: A Contribution to the Study of Jewish Origins* (Notre Dame: University of Notre Dame Press, 1977).

12

Hermeneutics:
From Ancient to
Contemporary Meaning

The word "hermeneutics" wears several hats.[1] In secular literature it is used to mean almost any aspect of interpretation. Even in biblical studies, in which it has the more technical definition as the process by which a later community finds contemporary significance in a text that comes from an earlier time, it can have different shades of meaning. In studies with a historical focus, it can refer to the identification of the principles of the interpretation of Scripture used by the ancient communities of faith. For example, we can identify the hermeneutical principles of Paul in his exegesis of the story of Abraham in Romans 4. Without the "s" the word hermeneutic can label a particular theory of interpretation that reached its height in the 1960s. Based on the philosophy of Martin Heiddegger, it is called the "new hermeneutic." As used in this chapter, hermeneutics refers to the process by which the preacher moves from the ancient meaning of a text to a statement of its contemporary relevance.

As in the case of some other disciplines, there is no normative approach. Two contemporary approaches seem to me to offer special promise to the preaching ministry. They are the hermeneutic of analogy and the hermeneutical program of Paul Ricoeur.[2]

Hermeneutic of Analogy

The hermeneutic of analogy is based on the notion that the change in cultural setting between the time of the Bible and contemporary life has created a "hermeneutical gap." That is, words, concepts, realities that had specific meanings in the ancient world may have quite different meanings today.[3]

Many of the Psalms assume that the earth is supported above a raging sea by mighty pillars. That makes great poetry but poor science. How do we interpret such passages so that they can have positive meaning for the modern community of faith?

In 1 Samuel 28, Saul goes to the medium of Endor for guidance. This visit is surprising because ". . . Saul had put the mediums and wizards out of the land" (1 Samuel 28:3). Even more surprising is the appearance of the dead Samuel through the ministry of the medium. Now the importance of the story to the contemporary church is hardly obvious. Even though we have Ouija boards and seances on church youth group retreats, no one takes their "messages" seriously.

The prophet Malachi quotes the Lord as being revulsed over the sacrifices brought to the altar of the rebuilt temple. ". . . You say, 'How have we despised thy name?' By offering polluted food upon my altar . . . blind animals . . . lame or sick . . ." (Malachi 1:6-8). Today animal sacrifice has disappeared from the life of the people of God. The same prophet laments the failure to bring the tithe. "Will man rob God? . . ." (3:8). Is the only pertinence of this text the fortification of the annual appeal of the stewardship committee?

A commonly shared, though debatable, conclusion of the quest of the historical Jesus is that he was known as an exorcist. But what sense can we make of exorcism in these psychologically sophisticated times?

Beginning with Matthew 21:28, we read a series of anti-Jewish parables. Are they justification for anti-Semitism?

In Acts 10, Peter is sent to the Gentile Cornelius and is given a vision which justifies the Gentile mission of the church. Since the main-line church today is made up of persons who are "Gentile" by the standards of Acts, are the implications of that mission exhausted?

In Colossians 3:18, we find the beginning of one of the famous household codes, "Wives, be subject to your husbands . . ." Despite debate over the precise meaning of the verb "be subject" and the fact that such prescriptions contain no peculiar Christian doctrine, the sense of the passage is unfortunately clear. Do we write off such passages as antique or perhaps excise them from the canon; or, gulp, do we pass them out like prescription medicine?

The hermeneutic of analogy seeks both to take account of the changed cultural situation and to maintain a sense of continuity between the traditional and contemporary meaning. It acknowledges the differences between old and new communities, yet affirms sufficient similarities that the biblical traditions can speak appropriately.

The basis of the similarity is that of *analogous experience* in ancient and contemporary settings. While cultural forms and expressions change, there are underlying currents of experience which are much the same, even though they may have different names. The hermeneutic of analogy seeks to identify realities, experiences, and/or forces in our world that are analogous to those in the biblical world. The key is the identification of realities (sacred and secular) which *function* in our world analogously to those of the biblical world.

To the ancient community of Israel, the figure of the raging sea represented the power of chaos which sought to overthrow the order of the cosmos. The pillars of the deep, therefore, were a figure used to affirm that the power of. God had overcome the threat of chaos by raising the earth above the raging sea. The hermeneutic of analogy asks, "What functions to threaten us in a way similar to the way the raging sea threatened Israel? What are our 'pillars of the deep,' that is, how do we experience the power of chaos being overcome?"

A medium, like the witch of Endor, provided direct, unambiguous answers to life's problems. What is the modern analogue of the medium? To whom do we turn for guidance in much the same way as Saul? Few in the main-line church take the Ouija board seriously, but what about the guidance we seek in self-help books and groups full of "pop" psychology but devoid of the gospel?

As in the case of the community to which Malachi wrote, worship is still the center of the life of the people of God. While we no longer practice animal sacrifice, we might well bring polluted food and unfit offerings to the altar. I have preached some sermons that were as lame as a calf with a broken leg. A useful index of the quality of our sacrifices is the ethical life of the church. In ancient Israel when worship was vigorous and strong, the life of the community tended to be vigorous and strong. The inverse was true when worship was corrupt.

What was the function of the tithe in Israel? Among other things, it symbolically dramatized the commitment of the worshiper to the whole community. The tithe was the basis of the support of the priesthood and the temple (which were regarded as life-giving institutions) and the poor. Further, the offering of the tithe was a symbolic declaration that God was the absolute owner of the universe and that the worshiper recognized himself or herself as a steward of the resources of God, resources which were to be used in behalf of the whole community. What analogous actions by the contemporary church can dramatize such values and commitments today? How can we "bring the full tithe into the storehouse"?

The exorcism at Capernaum in Mark 1:21-28 is centered in the figure of a demoniac who comes into contact with the power of Jesus. What functions in the contemporary world in the same way as the experience of demon possession in the story? The demon represents forces that bind and restrict human life. It replaces conscious choice with destructive personal and social result. Neill Hamilton speaks of "social equivalents of possession," social forces which result in crippling and destructive behavior, such as the compulsion to work, the compulsion to consume, the objectification of other persons in the compulsion for sex. Against such compulsions are the values and power of Jesus, "the stronger one."[4]

The parables of Matthew 21 were put into their present form by a church which was in the position of a sect swimming against the current of main-line Judaism. If I look for analogous groups in modern life, the main-line church is in a position comparable to that of Judaism in the world of Matthew. It is a part of the dominant culture. In the Gospels, the parables challenge not Judaism *per se* but religiosity which does not embrace the values and ethics of the royal rule of God. Indeed, the contemporary church is hardly the place to find the equivalents of tax collectors and harlots. This suggests that the parables, far from being a legitimation of anti-Semitism, should be read as a device for calling the church into question. What is the soiled robe we wear to the feast?

In the story of Peter and Cornelius, the basic functional reality is the well-known separation between Jewish and Gentile communities. Luke uses the story to say that the fold of the people of God is being enlarged to include Gentiles. In the modern era, as noted, already the church is in a position similar to that of the Jewish religious community that Luke caricatures. The hermeneutic of analogy asks, "Who in our culture are the functional correspondents of the Gentiles in the ancient setting? How is God enlarging the fold today?"

This hermeneutic may offer a way to deal with some passages like Colossians 3:1ff. In the ancient world the function of such commands may have been to help strengthen the social fabric of the community against collapse.[5] The hermeneutic of analogy asks, "What is important to increase the strength of the human community today?" The enforcement of such submission would lead precisely to the social chaos which the code was intended to guard against! Therefore, to achieve the same function, one would preach a gospel of liberation.

Paul Ricoeur: The New Colossus

The hermeneutical theory of Paul Ricoeur is becoming as canonical to the present generation of biblical scholars as was the demythologizing program of Rudolf Bultmann a generation ago. In lifting up an aspect of Ricoeur's program which is especially relevant for preaching, I draw in a very small bucket from a very deep well.

An important dimension of Ricoeur's program is the idea that once a text leaves the hand of its author, it has a life of its own, quite independent of the meaning the author intended. The meaning

of the text can be determined only by looking at the text itself;[6] and
the meaning one finds will be determined, in no small part, by one's
own situation. Thus, a text has a "surplus of meaning," that is,
more meaning than can be mined at any one time. This accounts
for the experience of returning to a text that is as familiar as one's
Phila.6664 American Politics & Christian Ethics
favorite campsite and finding a new shopping center there.

Further, the form of a text and its meaning cannot be divorced.
The form of a text determines the character of the interaction between
text and recipient. A narrative, for instance, is not just a literary
device. It is a form that orients the listener to receive the text in a
certain way. A poem is received differently by the listener than is
a narrative.[7] Although one can "explain" the meaning of a narrative,
the narrative itself is much richer than the explanation.

For Ricoeur, the most important aspect of interpretation lies not
in establishing what a text meant in its historical setting but in
making an account of what it means to the contemporary audience.[8]
For this he proposes a three-phrase hermeneutical movement: (1)
recognizing the first naiveté; (2) arousing the critical consciousness;
and (3) returning to the text in a second naiveté.

At the level of the first naiveté, we take the meaning of the text
for granted. We do not question its view of the world, its language,
its imagery. Symbolism is often mistaken for a literal view of reality.

For instance, Genesis 3 is naively read as a factual account of an
event that took place in a particular garden in the ancient Near East.
In the form of a snake (which had legs when the chapter opened)
the devil came to a woman and enticed her to eat a piece of fruit
from a special tree. In retaliation, God cursed the woman because
of her disobedience.

When the critical consciousness is aroused, we recognize the
historical and cultural distance between the text and us. We realize
that we do not see things today as people did three millenia ago,
and we develop a sense of alienation from the text. In the terminology
of Ricoeur, we engage in a "hermeneutic of suspicion" in which
we raise questions about the language, imagery, and symbolism of
the text.[9] We take an almost jaundiced view of the text.

In Genesis 3, we question whether the woman and the man were flesh-and-blood persons. The narrative does not really say that the snake is the devil. In any case, how could people hear "the sound of the Lord God walking in the garden?" That sounds like anthropomorphizing of the most blatant kind. Yet is it clear that God's judgment falls on both the man and the woman.

The important function of the critical consciousness is to destroy our sense of cozy familiarity with the text. In the first naiveté, we think we know what a text means, and that knowledge interferes with the possibility of hearing the text afresh. When we are sufficiently distanced from the text, we can return to it.

While the critical consciousness thus performs the important function of clearing the underbrush from the thicket of our perception, it does not re-sod the clearing. It leaves the forest floor bare. In order to fill the void of meaning, we return to the text in the second naiveté.

In the second naiveté, we appropriate the language and symbolism of the text, but we do so recognizing its authentic character.[10] In an act of conscious choice, we give ourselves to the text. The advantage of the critical consciousness is that we no longer confuse symbol and fact. In the second naiveté, the symbol is able to open to us aspects of reality to which we would otherwise have no access.

Thus, I realize that Genesis 3 is a mythic story which interprets certain aspects of reality. It is not intended to provide a historical report which would satisfy the curiosity of the staff of "60 Minutes." Instead, its purpose is to give a theological explanation of why the world is fractured and broken. Thus, I can speak about "the Fall" as if it were a specific historical event, realizing that the truth of the story is not dependent on the historicity of the events described in the text. I can speak of God walking in the cool of the garden without making the mistake of thinking that the symbol and the reality are the same.

Ted Peters sees three homiletical moments corresponding to the three phases of the hermeneutical movement.[11] Preaching in the first naiveté is simple and concrete. Its purpose is to help build confidence in the traditional symbols of the Christian faith, making them come alive for the congregation. At the level of critical consciousness, preaching attempts to create a sense of distance between the congregation and the text. It raises tough questions about the adequacy of the congregation's traditional (and often chummy) understanding of the text. In the second naiveté the preaching reconstructs a symbolic world out of which the congregation can live.

This three-phase process may take place in a single sermon or a single sermon may be concerned with a single phase. In a balanced program of parish preaching, all three phases should receive significant attention because main-line congregations contain persons who need each (and different) phases. Many in the congregation need to be fed at their particular level of awareness while many need to be creatively challenged to move to the next phase.

To preach only one phase can warp a congregation (and a preacher). For example, to be always in the phase of critical consciousness would leave the congregation without a framework within which to understand its life and to make important ethical decisions. Consciously to give attention to the whole hermeneutical movement is to honor congregation and text.

Key Questions

1. The analogical questions:
   a. What are the basic realities in this text?
   b. What realities in our world function in the same way as those in the text?
2. The questions of Ricoeur:
   a. What do we naïvely take to be the meaning of this text?
   b. As we put the text into the fire of critical consciousness, how is our naïve understanding challenged?
   c. As we return to the text in a second naiveté, what do we apprehend that can form and shape our world?

Case Study: Revelation 13:11-18

1. The analogical questions:

a. What are the basic realities in this text? As I investigate the setting of Revelation, I find that the world of the text was one of conflict between the church and the persecuting power of Rome.

This beast is probably a pictorial representation of the imperial cult of the Roman empire in which the emperor was worshiped as a god. In the Roman world, this cult was fused with the government in such a way that religion was used to support the policies of the state.[12] For John, Rome (and Roman religion) is a personification of evil. This beast is deceptive because it masquerades like the lamb (Revelation 13:11), works miracles similar to those of the lamb (v. 13) and evokes worship (vv. 12, 15). Yet, while it looks and acts like the lamb, it speaks with the voice of a dragon and is identified by the evil number 666. Thus, a basic reality of this text is the power of evil. The text exposes how it operates: evil appears to offer goodness, when in fact it offers falsehood and the way to death.

 b. What realities in our world function in the same way as those in the text? What in our world uses religious motifs to offer good but in fact leads to evil? I think of the ways in which the advertising industry sells us not only products but a world view at the center of which is the self-satisfaction of the individual through the consumption of goods and services. These days the advertising industry makes as much (or more) use of traditional religious language than some in the modern church who seem to be more comfortable with the language of human potential, class analysis, or business management than with the language of Zion. The peculiar amalgam of religion and government in the United States, symbolized by the motto "In God We Trust" on our coins, sometimes functions this way: in the name of God-given freedom, we built a weapons arsenal which could destroy the human race as quickly as a tissue burns in a roaring fire. The lay of the land of civil religion is well known. Lest I feel too smug, however, I remember occasions when, desperate to get a job done at church, I have left the impression with lay people that institutional maintenance is doing the complete will of God. The result was that jobs like cleaning the grease trap in the kitchen have short-circuited the potentially powerful witness of the laity in the larger society.

 2. The questions of Ricoeur:
 a. What do we naively take to be the meaning of this text? If one

is a typical main-line North American Protestant, one may think
that the text is too remote to be understood. If one has had any
exposure to the text, that exposure is likely to have come through
premillenialism. In the hands of its most widely known exponent,
Hal Lindsay, Revelation is seen as a blueprint of events leading up
to "the end." In this blueprint the beast of 13:11-18 is the "pal"
of the Antichrist. This pal is a "false prophet" which Lindsay
understands to mean a massive world religion whose Christology
has the spine of toothpaste.[13] If historically informed, one may be
aware that the symbol stands for the religion of emperor worship in
the Roman empire.

   b. *As we put the text into the fire of critical consciousness, how
is our naive understanding of the text challenged?* The more I read
Revelation, the more difficult it becomes. The blades of thought
which propel premillenialism are broken in half when one realizes
that the words had a meaning peculiar to the time of John. And if
the symbol had a concrete referent in the first century, why should
it mean anything else today?

   c. *As we return to the text in the second naiveté, what do we
apprehend that can form and shape our world?* Although the text
is rooted in a specific historical moment, it seems to describe in
almost mythical language experience which goes beyond that moment. Even that which is false and evil attempts to evoke from us
a sense of ultimacy and devotion (worship). In the full context of
Revelation I learn that the end of such devotion is exactly the opposite
of what it promises. It promises security and life but results in
insecurity and death. Therefore, through the medium of the text, I
can help the congregation discern the deceptive nature of evil. The
purpose of such a sermon might be to create a "world" in which
the listeners come face to face with the power of evil in such a way
as to recognize it for what it is and how it works. In order to do
this, the preacher might draw upon contemporary images of evil at
work in the world. To do so would preserve integrity between the
ancient symbol and its contemporary communication.

Suggestions for Further Reading

   A foundational article to understanding much contemporary hermeneutical discussion is Krister Stendahl, "Biblical Theology, Con-

temporary," *The Interpreter's Dictionary of the Bible,* ed. George A. Buttrick (Nashville: Abingdon Press, 1964), vol. 2, pp. 418-432. An excellent overview of hermeneutical models is Raymond E. Brown, "Hermeneutics," *The Jerome Biblical Commentary,* ed. Raymond E. Brown, *et al.* (New York: Prentice Hall Inc., 1969), pp. 605-623. A more specialized introduction is James A. Sanders, "Hermeneutics," *The Interpreter's Dictionary of the Bible: Supplement,* ed. Keith Crim (Nashville: Abingdon Press, 1976), pp. 402-407. Ernest Best, *From Text to Sermon: Responsible Use of the New Testament in Preaching* (Atlanta: John Knox Press, 1978), demonstrates the inadequacy of many hermeneutical models but does not pose a strong positive alternative.

On the new hermeneutic see Paul J. Achtemeier, *An Introduction to the New Hermeneutic* (Philadelphia: The Westminster Press, 1969); *The New Hermeneutic,* ed. James M. Robinson and John B. Cobb (New York: Harper & Row Publishers, Inc., 1964); and Robert W. Funk, *Language, Hermeneutic, and Word of God* (New York: Harper & Row Publishers, Inc., 1966).

The bibliography of Paul Ricoeur is immense. Representative works through which one may enter the world of his thought include his "Biblical Hermeneutics," *Semeia* 4 (1975), pp. 29-145; *The Symbolism of Evil,* trans. Emerson Buchanan (Boston: Beacon Press, 1969); *Interpretation Theory: Discourse and the Surplus of Meaning* (Fort Worth: Texas Christian University Press, 1976); *Essays on Biblical Interpretation,* ed. Lewis S. Mudge (Philadelphia: Fortress Press, 1980). For a similar viewpoint, see Hans-Georg Gadamer, *Truth and Method* (New York: The Crossroad Publishing Co., 1982).

An identifiable hermeneutic is emerging from process theology. For examples see J. Gerald Janzen, "The Old Testament in Process Perspective," *Magnalia Dei,* ed. F. Cross, W. E. Lemke, P. D. Miller (New York: Doubleday Publishing Co., Inc., 1976), pp. 480-509; William A. Beardslee, *A House for Hope: A Study in Process and Biblical Thought* (Philadelphia: The Westminster Press, 1972); and a series of introductory articles that appeared in the *Journal of the American Academy of Religion* 47 (1979), no. 1.

Appendix

Compendium of Key Questions

The Historical Background (Chapter 3)
1. What level of the history of the text will inform the sermon?
2. The introductory questions:
   a. Who was the author of the text?
   b. Where was the text written?
   c. When was the text written?
   d. What was the situation for which the text was written?
   e. Why (for what purpose) was the text written?
3. What would it feel like to be in that situation?
4. Is it important for the congregation to experience something of the atmosphere and feeling of that situation in order to be receptive to the full force of the text?
5. When I read this text, what do I:
   a. See?
   b. Hear?
   c. Smell?
   d. Touch?

  e. Taste?
6. Is it important for the congregation to experience imaginatively any of these in order to feel the full force of the text?

Word Studies (Chapter 4)
1. What are the fulcrum words on which this text turns?
2. How would the listeners or readers to whom this text was originally addressed have heard those words?
3. Is there so much distance between the congregation and the fulcrum words that the words will need to be explained in order to communicate with vitality and concreteness?
4. How can I concretely and vividly convey the meaning of the words to the congregation?

Form Criticism: The Individual Threads (Chapter 5)
1. What form is this text?
2. What was the function of that form in the ancient community?
3. Does the function of the text suggest a thrust for the sermon?
4. Does the form of the text suggest a form for the sermon?

Redaction Criticism: The Whole Picture (Chapter 6)
1. Can we identify the approximate shape of the text before it reached the author's hand?
2. How has the author reshaped the tradition?
3. Does the literary context cast light on the interpretation of the text by the redactor?
   a. What comes before?
   b. What comes after?
   c. What is the effect of the placement of the text?
4. What are the central or significant motifs/words/persons in the pericope?
5. How are these significant elements used and what meaning do they have in the rest of the literature produced by the redactor?
6. In light of the reshaping, the context, and the meaning of the major motifs, how is the redactor addressing the community through the text?
7. What situation in the redactor's community might have called forth this address?

8. Does the community to which the sermon will be preached find itself in a similar situation?

9. Does the redactor's message appropriately address the community to which the sermon will be preached?

Structuralism: The Text Manifests Deep Structure (Chapter 7)

1. What are the basic units of the text?
2. What is the situation at the beginning of the text?
3. What is the situation at the end of the text?
4. What is the basic opposition underlying the text?
5. Do elements of the text evoke larger structures which have a role in the text?
6. What transformations take place as the text moves from beginning to end?
7. How does the underlying opposition and its resolution suggest structure and content for the sermon?

Sociological Exegesis: Text and Social Reality (Chapter 8)

1. Does the text or background about the text suggest that a description of some social fact(s) may be pertinent to the interpretation of the text?
2. Does the text or background reading suggest that an aspect of social history might be important to the interpretation of the text?
3. What was the social position of the community to which the text was addressed?
4. What was the social situation within the community to which the text was written?
5. What was the social strategy of the text? For example:
   a. Does it confirm the present situation?
   b. Does it ask the community to adjust to the present situation?
   c. Does it call for a reform of the present situation?
   d. Does it describe the replacement of the old order with a new?
6. What was the relationship between the social reality of the community to which the text was written and the language and symbolism of the text?
7. Is the congregation to which the sermon will be preached in

a social position that is similar or dissimilar to that of the
community to which the text was addressed?
8. Does the strategy of the text in its ancient setting suggest an
   appropriate social strategy toward which the sermon might
   aim?
9. Do the language and symbolism of the text suggest a function
   for the language and symbolism of the sermon?

Liberation Theology: Exegesis from Below (Chapter 9)
1. For its understanding, does this text presuppose awareness of
   an oppressive reality in a situation to which the text was
   directed?
2. Can we describe how oppression was manifest in the situation
   to which the text was directed?
3. Did the community to which this text was directed participate
   in the reality of oppression as the oppressed or as the oppressor?
4. What message did this text speak:
   a. To the oppressor?
   b. To the oppressed?
5. In the contemporary world, do we find oppressive situations
   similar to that/those of the text?
6. Does the congregation to which the sermon will be preached
   participate in oppression as the oppressed or as the oppressor?
7. In the contemporary setting what is necessary for liberation to
   be effected?
8. Can the preacher suggest some concrete ways in which the
   congregation can become a part of the movement toward liberation?

Interpreting a Biblical Text As a Work of Art (Chapter 10)
1. What feeling is expressed in this text?
2. How can that feeling be expressed adequately in a sermon?

Canonical Criticism: The Problem of Contemporary Authority
(Chapter 11)
1. What was the function of this text in the community to which
   it was addressed? (Pastoral support? Prophetic challenge?).
2. What is the theological thrust of the passage which is important

to the religious community beyond the situation to which the text was directed?

3. As I consider the situation of my congregation, are we in need of hearing the text as pastoral support or as prophetic challenge?

4. In order to hear this text appropriately, with whom do we identify?

Hermeneutics: From Ancient to Contemporary Meaning (Chapter 12)

1. The analogical questions:
   a. What are the basic realities in this text?
   b. What realities in our world function in the same way as those in the text?

2. The questions of Ricoeur:
   a. What do we naïvely take to be the meaning of this text?
   b. As we put the text into the fire of critical consciousness, how is our naïve understanding challenged?
   c. As we return to the text in the second naiveté, what do we apprehend that can form and shape our world?

Notes

[1]Gottwald properly warns against a theology of "God-in-the-gaps" in which God is used to explain data for which the reseacher has no other explanation, "Sociological Criticism of the Old Testament," *The Christian Century* 99 (1982), p. 477. For his reconstruction, see his *The Tribes of Yahweh* (Maryknoll: Orbis Books, 1979).

Chapter 1 (The Changing Situation in Sermon Preparation)

[1]At one Ivy League seminary, I observed students preparing for the content exams by reading religious comic books and memorizing flash cards as much as by reading the Bible.

[2]This situation is improving with the appearance of resources like the Proclamation Series (Fortress Press), the Knox Preaching Guides, the Interpretation Commentary series (both published by John Knox Press) and occasional individual volumes. The depth and success of the contributions are quite uneven.

[3]George M. Landes and Walter P. Wink, *The Nature and Methods of Biblical Exegesis* (New York: Union Theological Seminary, 1970), p. 21.

[4]Douglas Stuart, *Old Testament Exegesis: A Primer for Students and Pastors* (Philadelphia: The Westminster Press, 1980), p. 55. Copyright 1980 The Westminster Press. Used by permission.

[5]Other important movements in biblical exegesis which are promising for preaching include:

a. Rhetorical criticism. See *Rhetorical Criticism: Essays in Honor of James Muilenburg* ed. Jared J. Jackson and Martin Kessler (Pittsburgh: The Pickwick Press, 1974); and Joanna Dewey, *The Markan Public Debate: Literary Technique, Concentric Structure and Theology in Mark 2:1-3:6* (Chico: Scholars Press, 1980).

b. Tradition criticism. See Douglas Knight, *Rediscovering the Traditions of Israel*

(Missoula: Scholar's, 1973); *Tradition and Theology in the Old Testament,* ed. Douglas A. Knight (Philadelphia: Fortress Press, 1977)

c. Using psychological categories as a point of entry into the text. See Mary Ann Tolbert, *Perspectives on the Parables: An Approach to Multiple Interpretations* (Philadelphia: Fortress Press, 1978); Richard L. Rubenstein, *My Brother Paul* (New York: Harper & Row Publishers, Inc., 1972); Robin Scroggs, *Paul for a New Day* (Philadelphia: Fortress Press, 1977).

d. Phenomenology. Basic works are still the difficult writings of Edmund Husserl and Max Scheler. Other works of an introductory nature include Gerardus van der Leeuw, *Religion in Essence and Manifestation, A Study in Phenomenology* (Magnolia, Mass.: Peter Smith Publisher, Inc., 1963), 2 vols. Rudolf Otto, *The Idea of the Holy,* 2nd ed., trans. John W. Harvey (New York: Oxford University Press, 1958) as well as some of the writings of Paul Ricoeur. A theologian who has made extensive use of phenomenology is Edward Farley, *Ecclesial Man: A Social Phenomenology of Faith and Reality* (Philadelphia: Fortress Press, 1975) and *Ecclesial Reflection: An Anatomy of Theological Method* (Philadelphia: Fortress Press, 1982).

e. Literary criticism. Although its thrust is extremely promising for preaching, I have not devoted a separate chapter to literary criticism for two reasons: (1) many of the insights that would come from that discussion are similar to those raised by other disciplines; (2) by omitting that chapter, the length of the book is reduced sufficiently to make a substantial reduction in purchase price. Basic introductions to literary criticism can be found in William A. Beardslee, *Literary Criticism of the New Testament.* Edited by Dan O. Via, Jr. (Philadelphia: Fortress Press, 1970); Norman R. Petersen, *Literary Criticism for New Testament Critics.* Edited by Dan O. Via, Jr. (Philadelphia: Fortress Press, 1978); *Literary Interpretations of Biblical Narratives.* Edited by Kenneth R. Louis *et al.* (Nashville: Abingdon Press, 1974); *Literary Interpretations of Biblical Narratives II.* Edited by Kenneth R. Louis (Nashville: Abingdon Press, 1982).

Chapter 2 (Opening the Door to the World of the Text)

[1] Compare Karl Barth, "The Strange New World Within the Bible," in *The Word of God and the Word of Man,* trans. Douglas Horton (Magnolia, Mass., Peter Smith Publishers, Inc., 1958). Although I have adopted Barth's term, I have not followed his development of the theme in every particular.

[2] Fred B. Craddock, *Overhearing the Gospel* (Nashville: Abingdon Press, 1978), *passim.* Craddock develops this insight as part of his larger discussion of "overhearing" as a basic exegetical posture. *Overhearing the Gospel* and his *As One Without Authority* (Nashville: Abingdon Press, 1979) are among the most exciting pieces of homiletical literature today.

[3] Translation involves much more than simply rendering Hebrew, Aramaic, or Greek words with English equivalents. Genuine translation involves transferring the dynamic meaning and feeling of the first language into the second. Translation is thus fully accomplished only in the context of exegesis. Translators often unintentionally (but sometimes quite intentionally) overlay translations with their own theological presuppositions.

[4] On the oral interpretation of the Bible, I am grateful to correspondence with Gilbert L. Bartholomew.

[5] Of course the author of Hebrews 4:12 hardly had canon or sermon in mind when speaking of "the word of God."

Chapter 3 (The Historical Background)

[1] In order to pursue these questions, pastors will need an up-to-date introduction to both testaments. They may need also to consult appropriate entries in Bible dictionaries as well as the introductory sections of the commentaries. Because modern scholars write with an eye toward making a convincing case for their particular lines of interpretation, we need to be aware of the wheels of bias on which their axes are ground.

[2] J. Alberts Soggin, *Joshua, a Commentary*, trans. R. A. Wilson (Philadelphia: The Westminster Press, 1972), pp. 82-86.

[3] As supported by the many New Testament meanings of baptism, for example, as an entrance rite into the reign of God, as the forgiveness of sins, and as dying and rising with Christ, among others.

[4] Two other important hypotheses concerning the image are: (1) a reference to the custom of preparing a road over which a victorious king would travel; and (2) a reference to the Exodus from Egypt. The latter motif appears repeatedly throughout the book.

[5] James Muilenburg, "Introduction and Exegesis to Isaiah 40-66," *The Interpreter's Bible*. Edited by George A. Buttrick, *et al.* (Nashville: Abingdon Press, 1956), vol. 5, pp. 422ff. Compare Claus Westermann, *Isaiah Forty to Sixty-Six: A Commentary*, trans. David M. Stalker (Philadelphia: The Westminster Press, 1969), pp. 31ff.; John L. McKenzie, *Second Isaiah* (New York: Doubleday Publishing Co., Inc., 1968), pp. 15ff.

Chapter 4 (Word Studies)

[1] Edmund Steimle, "The Fabric of the Sermon," *Preaching the Story*, ed. Edmund Steimle *et al.* (Philadelphia: Fortress Press, 1980), p. 173, to whom I am indebted in the following.

[2] F. Bueschel, *"luo,"* Theological Dictionary of the New Testament (abbreviated *TDNT*), Edited by Gerhard Kittell and Gerhard Friedrich (Grand Rapids: Wm. B. Eerdmans Publishing Co., 1964), vol. 1, p. 352.

[3] W. Grundmann, *"hamartano,"* *TDNT*, vol. 1, p. 293.

[4] Or "May YHWH save."

[5] We should not press the theological relationship between the name Jesus and the name Joshua because Jesus was a common name in the first century.

[6] For example Gerhard Von Rad, *Genesis, a Commentary*, rev. ed. (Philadelphia: The Westminster Press, 1973), p. 265.

[7] Or "God strives." The etymology of Israel indicates it may have originally meant "may God rule," *ibid.*, p. 322.

[8] F. Hauck and G. Bertram, *"makarios,"* *TDNT*, vol. 3, pp. 362-370; J. Y. Campbell, "Blessedness," *The Interpreter's Dictionary of the Bible* (abbreviated *IDB*). Edited by George A. Buttrick *et al.* (Nashville: Abingdon Press, 1964), vol. 1, pp. 445-446; L. Mowry, "Beatitude," *IDB*, vol. 1, pp. 369-371.

[9] For example, F. W. Beare, *The Gospel According to Matthew: Translation, Commentary, and Notes* (New York: Harper & Row Publishers, Inc., 1982); I. Howard Marshall, *The Gospel of Luke* (Grand Rapids: Wm. B. Eerdmans Publishing Co., 1978), pp. 248-250.

[10] F. Hauck and E. Bammel, *"ptochos,"* *TDNT*, vol. I, pp. 883-915; C. U. Wolf, "poor," *IDB*, vol. III, pp. 843-844; L. E. Keck, "poor," *IDB* (Supplement), pp. 672-675.

[11] For example J. C. Fenton, *Saint Matthew* (Philadelphia: The Westminster Press, 1978), p. 80.

[12]IQM 14:7. Beyond the consensus that the Qumran community may have used "the poor" as a self-designation, the exact meaning of "poor" and "poor in spirit" is widely debated. For a clearly stated view opposing my own, see L. E. Keck, "poor," *IDB* (supplement), p. 673.

[13]In these examples the characters leave their possessions behind but do not put them in the service of human need.

[14]On this theme see Luke T. Johnson, *Sharing Possessions: Mandate and Symbol of Faith, No. 9.* Edited by Walter Brueggeman and John R. Donahue (Philadelphia: Fortress Press, 1981).

Chapter 5 (Form Criticism: The Individual Threads)

[1]Until the late 1960s, most form critics used the word "form" for two different references. In technical literature today, particularly in studies of Jewish literature, one finds the word "structure" referring to the outline or typical features of a text. The word "genre" refers more generally to the type of expression such as proverb, miracle story, diatribe. Thus a form critic might say, "This psalm is of the hymn genre and it has the structure of a community lament." A German word sometimes employed to refer to genre is *Gattung*.

[2]Gerhard Von Rad, *Genesis,* rev. ed., trans. John Marks (Philadelphia: The Westminster Press, 1972), p. 320.

[3]Among the studies which have led to this discovery are: Owen Barfield, *Poetic Diction: A Study in Meaning* (New York: Columbia University Press, 1973); Philip Wheelwright, *The Burning Fountain: A Study in the Language of Symbolism,* rev. ed. (Magnolia, Mass.: Peter Smith Publisher, Inc., 1983) and *Metaphor and Reality* (Bloomington: Indiana University Press, 1962); the many writings of Paul Ricoeur; Ernst Cassirer, *The Philosophy of Symbolic Forms,* trans. Ralph Manheim (New Haven: Yale University Press, 1957), 3 vols.; Susanne K. Langer, *Philosophy in a New Key: A Study in the Symbolism of Reason, Rite and Art* (Cambridge: Harvard University Press, 1957); Amos N. Wilder, *Early Christian Rhetoric: The Language of the Gospel* (Cambridge: Harvard University Press, 1971).

Chapter 6 (Redaction Criticism: The Whole Picture)

[1]Central components in the methodology of redaction criticism include examining the editorial composition of the document as well as isolating its characteristic themes and vocabulary. R. H. Stein identifies several compositional techniques used by Mark to shape the Second Gospel. These signs of editorial activity include seams, insertions, summaries, the creation of pericope, modification of material, omissions, arrangement, vocabulary, introduction, and conclusion of the work. "The Proper Methodology for Ascertaining a Markan Redaction History," *Novum Testamentum* 13 (1971), pp. 181-198. Similar methods are used by all who modify inherited material for their own purposes.

[2]Redaction criticism also allows us to treat themes from the perspective of their use in a whole work, for example, the notion of law in Matthew.

[3]Norman Perrin, *Rediscovering the Teachings of Jesus* (New York: Harper & Row Publishers, Inc., 1976), pp. 79-80. Others argue that Mark 2:18-20 contains more material from the historical Jesus.

[4]This can be traced in Eduard Schweizer, *The Good News According to Mark,* tran. Donald Madvig (Atlanta: John Knox Press, 1970), p. 67. Some interpreters regard verses 19*b* and 20 as a Markan creation.

[5] An introduction to canonical Jewish literature or a reliable commentary on Exodus will provide a capsule of the range of scholarly theories about "what" happened.

[6] The date of the poem, as well as its relationship to the longer Song of the Sea from the mouth of Moses (Exodus 15:1-18) is debated. I represent what I take to be the dominant and persuasive opinion.

[7] Norman K. Gottwald, *The Tribes of Yahweh: A Sociology of the Religion of Liberated Israel 1250-1050 B.C.* (Maryknoll: Orbis Books, 1979), pp. 117-119.

[8] The poem may be the result of a complex history of development, the tracing of which is beyond our present interest.

[9] Brevard S. Childs, *Introduction to the Old Testament as Scripture* (Philadelphia: Fortress Press, 1979), p. 176. Compare J. P. Hyatt, *Commentary on Exodus.* (Grand Rapids: Wm. B. Eerdmans Publishing Co., 1980), pp. 162ff.

[10] In the case of the Synoptic Gospels, the use of a synopsis will often cause an evangelist's particular emphasis to stand out. In the case of the Pentateuch and other narrative books of the Hebrew Bible, source analysis (which identifies the form of the tradition prior to falling into the hands of the redactor) is often readily available in the commentaries. This is also true of the prophets and wisdom literature, the literature of early Christianity and the Johannine literature.

[11] The methodology used in redaction criticism (see footnote 1, this chapter) will often help identify the earlier form of the tradition.

[12] We may need to pay attention to literary context which extends much further than the immediate placement of the text.

[13] This conclusion is reached by comparing Luke's setting with that of Matthew 22:1-10 and the Gospel of Thomas (Saying 64) as well as by noticing obvious Lukan themes. Compare John D. Crossan, *In Parables* (New York: Harper & Row Publishers, Inc., 1973), pp. 69-73, and I. H. Marshall, *The Gospel of Luke* (Grand Rapids: Wm. B. Eerdmans Publishing Co. 1978), pp. 584ff.

[14] Marshall, p. 587.

Chapter 7 (Structuralism: The Text Manifests Deep Structure)

[1] Structuralism is sometimes imprecisely referred to as "semiotic exegesis," a term with a specific technical meaning.

[2] Throughout I am indebted to the basic works of Daniel Patte, *What Is Structural Exegesis?* (Philadelphia: Fortress Press, 1976) and Daniel Patte and Aline Patte, *Structural Exegesis—from Theory to Practice: Exegesis of Mark 15 and 16 Hermeneutical Implications* (Philadelphia: Fortress Press, 1978) as well as *The New Testament and Structuralism: A Collection of Essays.* Edited and translated by Alfred M. Johnson, Jr. (Pittsburgh: The Pickwick Press, 1976) and *Structuralism and Biblical Hermeneutics.* Edited and translated by Alfred M. Johnson, Jr. (Pittsburgh: The Pickwick Press, 1979).

[3] Lexies are determined by factors like change of place, change of time, arrivals and departures, changes in the situation of characters, spoken lines. See Corina Galland, "Structural Readings: How to Do Them," *Structuralism and Biblical Hermeneutics,* pp. 189ff.

[4] A mytheme is a simple statement, rather like a lexie, which contains a single unit of thought or which represents a single action.

[5] In some cases the mythemes, represented by only one symbol, for instance $F_x(a)$, may combine several different characters or actions and are then referred to as a bundle of mythemes or a macromytheme.

[6] This model is the capstone of a six-step method of narrative analysis which may be

found in Jean Calloud, *Structural Analysis of Narrative*, trans. Daniel Patte (Philadelphia: Fortress Press, 1976).

[7] With some others I find potential historical and theological weaknesses in structuralism. In searching for the universal deep structure in the text, the structuralist will often bypass the historical context of the text and will even overlook the particular content. Indeed, structural analysis is often conducted for the sake of demonstrating the validity of structural theory rather than interpreting the text. For a constructive statement of the relationship between structuralism and the questions of history, see Alfred M. Johnson, Jr., "Structuralism, Biblical Hermeneutics and the Role of Structural Analysis in Historical Research," *Structuralism and Biblical Hermeneutics*, pp. 1-28. Further, when texts are emptied of content, their theological particularity is lost, and they become simply examples of general human phenomena.

[8] Although the actantial model of Greimas is not the source of any of these questions, it obviously could serve as a homiletical framework. The preacher would need to actualize the various actants in their interrelationship in the sermon.

[9] A structural analysis of this vignette is actually part of a structural exegesis of the larger Elijah cycle.

Chapter 8 (Sociological Exegesis: Text and Social Reality)

[1] The surveys of the history of research call attention to interest in the social reality of the biblical milieu in the early years of this century. Representative of the influential contributors are W. Robertson Smith, Johannes Pedersen, Adolf Deissmann and the "Chicago School" (Shirley Jackson Case, Shailer Matthews). While occasional individual scholars have given attention to the social world(s) of the Bible, large numbers have begun to do so only in the last decade. A work from which the contemporary period might be dated is E. A. Judge, *The Social Pattern of Christian Groups in the First Century* (London: Tyndale, 1960).

[2] A helpful overview of methods is Robin Scroggs, "The Sociological Interpretation of the New Testament: The Present State of Research," *New Testament Studies* 26 (1979), esp. pp. 171-179.

[3] For a compendium of the purposes of sociological study of Christian literature, on which this list is partially based, see Jonathan Z. Smith, "The Social Description of Early Christianity," *Religious Studies Review* 1 (1975), pp. 19-25.

[4] Ronald F. Hock, *The Social Context of Paul's Ministry: Tentmaking and Apostleship* (Philadelphia: Fortress Press, 1980).

[5] For example, Abraham J. Malherbe, *Social Aspects of Early Christianity* (Baton Rouge: Louisiana State University Press, 1977).

[6] Joachim Jeremias, *Jerusalem in the Time of Jesus: An Investigation into Economic and Social Conditions During the New Testament Period*, trans. F. H. and C. H. Cave (Philadelphia: Fortress Press, 1975), pp. 359-376.

[7] Gerd Theissen, *The Social Setting of Pauline Christianity: Essays on Corinth*, trans. John H. Schutz (Philadelphia: Fortress Press, 1982), pp. 147ff.

[8] So designated by John H. Elliot, *A Home for the Homeless* (Philadelphia: Fortress Press, 1982), pp. 10-11.

[9] James A. Wilde, "The Social World of Mark's Gospel," Society of Biblical Literature *Seminar Papers*. Edited by Paul Achtemeier (Chico: Scholars, 1978), vol. 2, pp. 47-70.

[10] "Judah" is a designation for the powerless group. Compare Paul D. Hanson, *The Dawn of Apocalyptic*, rev. ed. (Philadelphia: Fortress Press, 1979), pp. 325ff.

[11] Wayne Meeks, "The Man from Heaven in Johannine Sectarianism," *Journal of Biblical Literature* 91 (1972), pp. 44-72.

[12] Throughout I am indebted to John Elliot, *A Home for the Homeless*. I fully realize that his thesis is controversial.

Chapter 9 (Liberation Theology: Exegesis from Below)

[1] A component of liberation theology, especially as practiced in Third World settings, is class analysis after the fashion of Karl Marx.

[2] In the case of middle-class North American Christians, I find: the Bible to be a gold mine of treasure texts to support the work ethic; the idea that the fundamental purpose of religion is to help people to be ''good'' and to assist them with their problems; and the notion that religious experience is largely a matter of the heart so that ethics become a matter of private behavior. God is a hearty partner who wants us to achieve ''success'' according to standards defined by middle-class values.

[3] Because liberation is a powerful theme, it quickly began to be used in the first world as a way of describing almost any act of ministry from deliverance from alcohol to liberation from sin. While such uses are not unfitting, it is important to remember that liberation theology originated as a call for social and systemic justice.

[4] When preaching on prophetic literature from the liberation perspective, I think it is important for the preacher to identify not with the prophet but with the audience to which the text was spoken. In contemporary North American life, the preacher is not over-and-against the congregation; but because of participation in the social, economic, and political structures of the first world, the preacher is at one with the congregation under the word of the text.

[5] To be sure, the wisdom literature also extolls the virtues of affluence as in Ecclesiastes 10:9, but the wisdom literature contains its own critique of that viewpoint, as in Ecclesiastes 2:4-11.

[6] Paul D. Hanson, *The Dawn of Apocalyptic,* rev. ed. (Philadelphia: Fortress Press, 1979).

[7] Some claim that apocalyptic encourages a sense of passivity in the face of oppression. However, I am convinced that Christian apocalyptic is penetrated by the notion that the rule of God is manifesting itself in signs of liberation. The purpose of the community is to announce those signs, join in them, and even to work them. Note the ministry of the two witnesses in Revelation 11.

[8] See the remark of Peter Paris, cited by Peter Hodgson, *Children of Freedom: Black Liberation in Christian Perspective,* new ed. (Philadelphia: Fortress Press, 1974), p. 85, n. 39.

[9] Especially when first encountering liberation theology, pastors can easily fall into the trap of preaching only exposé and condemnation of first-world life.

[10] The history of the development of a text may reveal that it was spoken at different times to different situations.

[11] John Bright, *The History of Israel,* 3rd ed. (Philadelphia: The Westminster Press, 1981), pp. 324ff. and his *Jeremiah* (New York: Doubleday Publishing Co., Inc., 1965), pp. 137ff.; John A. Thompson, *The Book of Jeremiah* (Grand Rapids: Wm. B. Eerdmans Publishing Co., 1980), pp. 476ff.

Chapter 10 (Interpreting a Text As a Work of Art)

[1] The philosophy of art often uses the word ''form'' in the sense in which I use the words ''representation'' and ''embody.'' In this chapter I use the latter because of potential confusion between the uses of ''form'' in the philosophy of art and in form criticism.

²Susanne K. Langer, *Feeling and Form* (New York: The Scribner Book Companies, Inc., 1953), p. 40. Throughout I am indebted to Langer. I have given attention to similar themes in "Feeling and Form in Biblical Interpretation," *Encounter* 43 (1982), pp. 99-108; *Our Eyes Can Be Opened* (Washington: University Press of America, 1982), pp. 9-18; and "Shaping the Sermon by the Language of the Text," *Preaching Biblically*. Edited Don Wardlaw. (Philadelphia: The Westminster Press, 1983).

³Susanne K. Langer, *Philosophical Sketches* (Baltimore: Johns Hopkins University Press, 1962), p. 85.

⁴Susanne K. Langer, *Mind: An Essay on Human Feeling* (Baltimore: Johns Hopkins University Press, 1972), vol. 2, pp. 278-279.

⁵Susanne K. Langer, *Philosophy in a New Key: A Study in the Symbolism of Reason, Rite and Art,* 3rd ed. (Cambridge: Harvard University Press, 1957), pp. 150ff., *Mind,* vol. 2, pp. 301ff.

⁶Langer, *Feeling and Form,* p. 292. Mythic tales may have first been presented in dance and song (*Philosophy in a New Key,* p. 190).

⁷Langer, *Philosophy in a New Key,* p. 180.

⁸This by no means exhausts the meaning of the narrative. Indeed, Gerhard Von Rad, *Genesis, a Commentary,* rev. ed. (Philadelphia: The Westminster Press, 1973), pp. 232-240, wishes to minimize any connection to child sacrifice.

⁹Langer, *Philosophy in a New Key,* p. 143. Compare Sallie McFague, *Speaking in Parables: A Study in Metaphor and Theology* (Philadelphia: Fortress Press, 1975), pp. 50-62.

¹⁰I have chosen to discuss only a few images in the passage. I am indebted to Otto Kaiser, *Isaiah One to Twelve: A Commentary,* (Philadelphia: The Westminster Press, 1972), pp. 71-86 and R.B.Y. Scott, "Introduction and Exegesis to Isaiah 1-39," *The Interpreter's Bible,* ed. George A. Buttrick, *et al.* (Nashville: Abingdon Press, 1965), vol. 5, pp. 204-211.

Chapter 11 (Canonical Criticism: The Problem of Contemporary Authority)

¹It is important to distinguish between canonical criticism and the task of writing the history of the formation of the Jewish and Christian canons. The former is a mode of interpretation of the Bible. The latter accounts for why certain books were included or excluded in the collections now regarded as canonical. For examples of the latter see Robert M. Grant, *The Formation of the New Testament* (London: Hutchinson, 1965) and *The Canon and the Masorah of the Hebrew Bible,* ed. Sid Z. Leiman (New York: KTAV, 1974).

²Brevard S. Childs, *Biblical Theology in Crisis* (Philadelphia: The Westminster Press, 1970). Compare James D. Smart, *The Strange Silence of the Bible in the Church: A Study in Hermeneutics* (Philadelphia: The Westminster Press, 1970). Childs does not like the name "canonical criticism" because that sounds to him as though canonical criticism is simply one more method to be applied to the text. He prefers to speak of the "canonical perspective" as a total context within which the Bible is interpreted.

³*Biblical Theology in Crisis,* pp. 32-50. Compare with James D. Smart, *The Past, Present, and Future of Biblical Theology* (Philadelphia: The Westminster Press, 1979), questions whether the biblical theology movement was actually a movement.

⁴*Biblical Theology in Crisis,* pp. 61-87.

⁵I am throughout indebted to the writings of James A. Sanders, many of which emphasize this theme.

⁶James A. Sanders, "Hermeneutics," *The Interpreter's Dictionary of the Bible: Sup-*

plementary Volume. Edited by Keith R. Crim *et al*. (Nashville: Abingdon Press, 1976), p. 405. These correspond to the two main "hermeneutic axioms" in the Bible: (1) God as the giver of grace who keeps the divine promise and (2) God as free to create and judge, even the chosen people.

[7] Sanders often refers to this function as "constitutive."

[8] Brevard S. Childs, *Introduction to the Old Testament as Scripture* (Philadelphia: Fortress Press, 1979), pp. 150ff.

[9] *Ibid*., p. 632.

[10] I do not mean the popular distinction between "pastoral" as a syrupy "God loves you" theology and "prophetic" as angry denunciation. In true convenantal theology, the bestowal of identity carries with it significant ethical responsibilities; prophetic challenge hopes for the recovery of both ethical responsibility and covenantal identity, and hence, blessing.

[11] Brevard S. Childs, *Introduction to the Old Testament as Scripture*, p. 75. Childs would disagree with some of the proposals I have made. See "Multiple Possibilities for Preaching in Each Text," pp. xxff.

[12] *Ibid*., p. 410.

[13] Sanders, "Hermeneutics," p. 407; Compare James A. Sanders, *God Has a Story Too: Biblical Sermons in Context* (Philadelphia: Fortress Press, 1979), pp. 18ff. An important and related part of the hermeneutical movement is that of dynamic analogy to which attention is given in chapter 12.

[14] Sanders points out that prophetic challenge is not usually for use in individual pastoral care when the context calls for pastoral support. Neither is it apropos in the wake of communal tragedy, such as a flood.

[15] Sanders, *God Has a Story Too*, p. 77.

[16] As in the case of any good prophet, one can see the pastoral (constitutive) element. For if the people rebuild the temple, their situation will improve.

Chapter 12 (Hermeneutics: From Ancient to Contemporary Meaning)

[1] For an overview of the meaning of the word "hermeneutics," see Richard E. Palmer, *Hermeneutics: Interpretation Theory in Schleiermacher, Dilthey, Heidegger, and Gadamer* (Evanston: Northwestern University Press, 1969), pp. 3ff.

[2] Other hermeneutical approaches are in use, especially the method widely known as "prooftexting." This method violates the integrity of both text and contemporary community.

[3] On the hermeneutic of analogy I am indebted to N. Q. Hamilton, *Jesus for a No-God World* (Philadelphia: The Westminster Press, 1969), pp. 176ff., and the writings of James A. Sanders, for example "Hermeneutics," *The Interpreter's Dictionary of the Bible, Supplementary Volume*. Edited by Keith R. Crim (Nashville: Abingdon Press, 1976), p. 406, and James A. Sanders, *God Has a Story Too* (Philadelphia: Fortress Press, 1979), pp. 20-22. For a serious question about this hermeneutic, see David Buttrick, "Interpretation and Preaching," *Interpretation* 35 (1981), pp. 52-53, who charges that "parallels" always lead to homosexuality and the like.

[4] Neill Q. Hamilton, *The Recovery of the Protestant Adventure* (New York: The Seabury Press, Inc., 1981), pp. 85ff.

[5] This assertion is highly debatable. For first-century evidence of stress on the social fabric, see Markus Barth, *The Anchor Bible, Ephesians 4-6* (New York: Doubleday Publishing Co., Inc., 1974), pp. 655ff. On the general problem see James E. Crouch, *The Origin and Intention of the Colossian Haustafel* (Goettingen: Vandenhoeck and Ruprecht, 1972).

[6] Paul Ricoeur, *Interpretation Theory: Discourse and the Surplus of Meaning* (Fort Worth: Texas Christian University, 1976), pp. 25ff.

[7] This process is not entirely subjective. It is controlled by the text itself.

[8] Ricoeur, *Interpretation Theory,* pp. 32ff.

[9] In this aspect of the hermeneutical process, we question not only the text but also our own consciousness ("How can I know that I know?") In *Freud and Philosophy: An Essay on Interpretation,* trans. Denis Savage (New Haven: Yale University Press, 1970), Ricoeur applies the work of Marx, Nietzsche, and Freud to philosophical and religion language to show that religion writers sometimes use religious language as a cover under which to discuss themes like class struggle and oedipal conflict.

[10] For this act, Ricoeur speaks in language that is becoming classic in the guild of biblical scholars. He makes a "wager" that the symbol will give him a better understanding of reality if he follows it. Compare Paul Ricoeur, *The Symbolism of Evil,* trans. Emerson Buchanan (Boston: Beacon Press, 1969), pp. 355ff.

[11] Ted Peters, "Hermeneutics and Homiletics," *Dialog* 21 (1982) pp. 121-129.

[12] See G. B. Caird, *The Revelation of St. John the Divine* (New York: Harper & Row Publishers, Inc. 1966), p. 171; G. R. Beasley-Murray, *The Book of Revelation* (Grand Rapids: Wm. B. Eerdmans Publishing Co., 1981), p. 216.

[13] Hal Lindsey, *There's a New World Coming* (Eugene, Or.: Harvest House Publishers, Inc., 1973), pp. 191-195.

Index of Scripture References